Exciting new resource

C000111188

Thank you for an overwhelming respon:
Services Interview Questions You'll Most Li

We are excited to announce a complete revamp to the set of
RESTful Java Web Services interview questions in the Second
Edition. The new edition includes fresh 275 interview questions
spread across a wide range of topics. Some of the topics included
are:

REST Basics   *JSON*

JAX-RS   *Postman*

Spring REST   *Swagger*

The interview questions are representation of most popular
questions asked at technical interviews of leading software
companies. Along with these technical questions, this book
includes 75 HR interview questions. All the questions are followed
by detailed and self-explanatory solutions.

We, at Vibrant Publishers, are committed to publishing books that
are content-rich, concise and approachable enabling more readers
to read and make the fullest use of them. We hope this book
provides you the most enriching learning experience.

Should you have any questions or suggestions, feel free to email us
at reachus@vibrantpublishers.com

THIS BOOK IS AVAILABLE IN E-BOOK and PAPERBACK FORMAT.

This page is intentionally left blank

RESTful JAVA WEB SERVICES

INTERVIEW QUESTIONS
YOU'LL MOST LIKELY BE ASKED

275

Interview Questions

VIBRANT
P U B L I S H E R S

RESTful Java Web Services

Interview Questions
You'll Most Likely Be Asked

ISBN-10: 1-949395-49-9
ISBN-13: 978-1-949395-49-5

Library of Congress Control Number: 2011912657

This publication is designed to provide accurate and authoritative information in regard to the subject matter covered. The author has made every effort in the preparation of this book to ensure the accuracy of the information. However, information in this book is sold without warranty either expressed or implied. The Author or the Publisher will not be liable for any damages caused or alleged to be caused either directly or indirectly by this book.

Vibrant Publishers books are available at special quantity discount for sales promotions, or for use in corporate training programs. For more information please write to **bulkorders@vibrantpublishers.com**

Please email feedback / corrections (technical, grammatical or spelling) to **spellerrors@vibrantpublishers.com**

To access the complete catalogue of Vibrant Publishers, visit **www.vibrantpublishers.com**

Contributors to this book:

RESTful Java Questions: Reshma Bidikar

 Reshma is a passionate Java engineer and educator. She has over 16 years experience in the IT industry working as a Senior Java Developer/Architect. Reshma has worked on technologies like Core Java, Spring, Hibernate, REST, JDBC to name a few. She has a Bachelor in Engineering degree in Computer Science. Currently she works full time as a freelance Java developer and corporate trainer.

Human Resource Questions: Nicole Farley

Nicole has more than a decade experience in retail management and new-hire training for start-ups to fortune-500 companies. She has conducted lot of interviews herself in her professional career working and consulting for her clients. Nicole lives in Kansas City and loves to blog during her free-time.

This page is intentionally left blank

Table of Contents

RESTful **Java Web Services** Interview Questions

Review these typical interview questions and think about how you would answer them. Read the answers listed; you will find best possible answers along with strategies and suggestions.

This page is intentionally left blank

Chapter **1**

Introduction to REST

1: What is REST?

Answer:

REST stands for REpresentational State Transfer. It is an architectural style for developing web services. In a REST application, the REST server exposes various services and client applications access those services. It makes use of the HTTP protocol, so the REST client and server communicate via HTTP. The data exchanged between the client and server can be in different formats like plain text, XML, HTML or JSON. So, a REST client requests a REST service via a URI, the REST service processes the client request and sends back the data in the appropriate format.

2: Which are the six principles on which REST API is based?

Answer:

a) **Client server** – Concerns should be separated between clients and servers. This allows client and server applications to be developed independently.

b) **Stateless** – The communication between the client and server should be stateless. The server need not remember the state of the client.

c) **Layered System** – Layered system simply means there can be several layers on the server side, but the client application need not be aware of this. So, your server code may be on one machine, database on another, etc. Multiple hierarchies such as gateways, firewalls, proxies can also be present between the client and server.

d) **Cache** – Responses from the server should be cacheable where possible in order to improve performance for the client.

e) **Uniform Interface** – The services provided by a REST application must be exposed via URIs. All interactions between client, server and intermediary components are based on the uniformity of their interfaces.

f) **Code on demand** – In addition to static data like XML or JSON, the REST application can send code like JavaScript, Applets which can be downloaded and executed by client applications.

3: Why is a REST service considered stateless?

Answer:

A REST application uses the HTTP protocol. HTTP is considered to be stateless. Statelessness simply means that the server does not store any state information about the client application. So, a client application needs to send all possible data that the server will require in order to process the client request. If at all the application needs to store some state specific data, this needs to be stored on the client side and sent with each HTTP request. At the server side, each HTTP request is processed independently.

4: Explain the differences between SOAP and REST.

Answer:

Both SOAP and REST technologies are used to create web services. However, there are some differences between the two:

a) SOAP is a protocol like HTTP whereas REST is an architectural style for developing web services - it can use any underlying protocol.

b) Though REST applications mostly use HTTP as the underlying protocol, they can use SOAP as well. However, a SOAP application cannot use REST.

c) SOAP uses the JAX-WS Java API, REST uses the JAX-RS Java API.

d) SOAP application provides its services via a WSDL file. A REST application, on the other hand, exposes its services using URIs.

e) When SOAP is used, only XML data format can be used. When REST is used, you can use XML, JSON, HTML or plain text as the data format.

5: What are the steps in building a RESTful API?

Answer:

The following are the steps involved in building a RESTful application:

a) **Identify resources** – Central to REST are resources. We need to model resources that are of interest to the consumers.

b) **Identify endpoints** – Next, we need to design URIs that map resources to endpoints.

c) **Identity actions** – We need to identity the HTTP methods that can be used to perform operations on the resources.

d) **Identity responses** – We need to identify the supported resource representation for the request and response along with the right status code to be returned.

6: What are the benefits of using a REST API?

Answer:

REST is an architectural style. It has several features that make it very powerful and easy to use:

a) It is independent of language or technology. So, the REST server can be written in any programming language and the REST client can be written in any programming language.

b) It is platform independent. So, the server can be on any operating system like Windows, Unix, etc. and the client can be on a different operating system.

c) It allows the application to scale easily. Since the client and server side are developed separately, each side can be scaled easily without affecting the other.

7: Explain the HATEOAS principle in REST with an example.

Answer:

HATEOAS stands for Hypermedia As The Engine Of Application State. This principle allows embedding links to other resources or services in a REST response. So, the REST client need not know about the services provided by a REST application. As and when the client requests information, along with information, the server provides links to other services that the client can access. Consider the following REST request which queries a REST service for employee information:

GET /employees/123

This will return a response as follows:

```
<employee>
    <employee_id>123</employee_id>
    <name>John Smith</name>
 <department>Admin</department>
    <link rel="payroll"
href="/employees/123/payroll" />
</employee>
```

So, along with the employee information, a link is provided which can be used by the client application to fetch payroll information for the employee.

8: How is a REST application different from an ordinary web application?

Answer:

Just like an ordinary web application, a REST application uses the HTTP protocol for the communication between the client and server application. However, there are couple of differences between the two:

a) Normally, a web application serves content in HTML
    format. A REST application can serve content in XML, JSON
    or HTML format.

b) The end users of a web application are humans who access
    the web application via their browsers. Though a REST
    application may be accessed via a browser for testing
    purpose, they are generally used by software applications
    itself which are known as REST clients.

9: Explain the principles of the Uniform Interface constraint.

Answer:

The Uniform Interface principle states that there should be a
uniform interface between clients and servers. It consists of the
following four principles:

a) **Resource identification** – Resource needs to be identified. A
    URI needs to be provided in order to identify and access a
    resource.

b) **Resource representation** – The resource needs to be
    serialized into a representation before being sent to a client.

c) **Self-descriptive messages** – Each message sent to the client
    needs to have information about how that message should
    be processed.

d) **HATEOAS** – Hypermedia As The Engine Of Application
    State (HATEOAS) allows embedding links to other
    resources or services provided by a REST server in a REST
    response.

10: What does the term "messaging" refer to in the context of a REST application?

Answer:

In a REST application, the client and the server communicate with each other via the HTTP protocol. So, the client application sends an HTTP request and the REST server sends an HTTP response. This is referred to as messaging. Each message consists of the message data and metadata, that is data about the message data. So, an HTTP Request consists of the HTTP Method being requested, parameters if any and request headers which is the metadata. So, also an HTTP Response consists of the Response Headers and actual data being requested.

This page is intentionally left blank

Chapter **2**

REST Resources, HTTP Methods and Status Codes

11: What is a resource in REST?

Answer:

Resource is a fundamental concept in REST. A resource is anything that can be accessed or manipulated by a client application. Examples of resources are html pages, text files, videos, images, etc. Each resource is identified via a URI. So, a REST server exposes a resource via a URI. The client application uses the URI of a resource to access it. The resource can be sent to the client application in a number of formats like HTML, XML or JSON. A resource can be related to another resource. For example, in a shopping application, a customer can place an order for any number of products. In this scenario, the product resource is related to the order resource.

12: Explain URI in the context of a REST application.

Answer:

Before a client application can use a service, it needs to be identified. URI which stands for Uniform Resource Identifier can be used to uniquely identify a resource in a REST application. So, it can be used to locate a resource on a server where the web service is hosted. It is of the following format:

`protocol://servername/resourcename`

Here,

`protocol` specifies the protocol used for communication. This is generally HTTP.

`servername` specifies the name of the server.

`resourcename` is used to identify the resource.

An example is `http://personservice.com/getperson`

13: Name the HTTP methods used by REST and explain each method.

Answer:

The following HTTP methods are used by REST:

  a) **GET** – This is used to retrieve some information. The URI of the request resource is specified.

  b) **POST** – The POST method is used to submit some information to the REST server. The information to be submitted should be sent along with the POST request.

  c) **HEAD** – This is used to retrieve metadata information about a resource.

  d) **DELETE** – This is used to request a resource to be deleted.

  e) **PUT** – This is used to update a resource. The URI of the resource to be updated needs to be specified.

f) **PATCH** – This is used to partially update a resource.

14: What does an HTTP request consist of?

Answer:

A REST application uses the HTTP protocol for communication between a client and server application. An HTTP request consists of the following:

a) HTTP method being invoked – Examples are GET, POST, PUT, HEAD, DELETE, etc.

b) The location of the resource (This is generally a URI).

c) HTTP request headers like Accept-Language, Accept-Encoding, etc. which specify the language or the encoding that the client can understand.

d) Message body (This is optional; it can be HTML, XML, JSON or even plain text).

15: What do the terms "Safety" and Idempotency" mean in the context of the HTTP methods used in a REST application?

Answer:

a) **Safety** – An HTTP method is considered to be safe if it does not modify the server state. The GET and HEAD methods are considered to be safe. These are used to retrieve information from the server and are implemented as read only operations without causing any changes to the server's state.

b) **Idempotency** – An HTTP method is considered to be idempotent if it does not change the server state when the operation is applied multiple times. The HTTP methods –

GET, HEAD, PUT and DELETE are idempotent. So, these methods will produce the same results even if they are applied multiple times. The POST method on the other hand is not idempotent as it can change the state of the server if invoked multiple times.

16: What is the use of the HTTP HEAD method?

Answer:

The HEAD method allows a client to only retrieve the metadata associated with a resource. The resource representation is not sent to the client. On several occasions, a client would like to check if a particular resource exists and doesn't really care about the actual data. In some scenarios, clients may like to know if a newer version of a resource is available before it downloads it. In both cases, a GET method could be "heavyweight" in terms of bandwidth and resources. Instead, a HEAD method is more appropriate since it only sends the header information. The HTTP header information is the same irrespective of whether it is a HEAD or a GET request. The client can then use this metadata information as required.

17: What is the difference between HTTP POST and PUT methods?

Answer:

Both the PUT and POST methods are used to change a resource on the server side. However, there are some differences between the two as follows:

a) POST is used to send data to the server. It is up to the REST service to decide what to do with the data. So, it can create a new resource with the data or store the data somewhere.

PUT on the other hand is used to update a resource. So, it "PUTs" the resource at the specified URI. If a resource already exists at that URI, it simply updates it.

b) PUT method is idempotent. So, even if it is invoked several times, it will simply keep updating the resource at the location specified; it will not change the state of the resource. The POST method, on the other hand, is not idempotent. So, if data is sent via a POST request to a server more than once, it might result in duplicate data on the server.

18: Explain the categories of the HTTP status codes.

Answer:

HTTP status codes are grouped into the following categories:

a) **Informational codes** – These belong to the 100 series. These indicate that the server has received the request but hasn't completed processing it.

b) **Success codes** – These belong to the 200 series. These indicate that the request has been received and processed successfully.

c) **Redirection codes** – These belong to the 300 series. These indicate that the request has been received but the client must perform an additional action to complete the request.

d) **Client error codes** – These belong to the 400 series. These indicate that there is an error on the client side.

e) **Server error codes** – These belong to the 500 series. These indicate that there is an error on the server side.

19: What is the HTTP status code 401 used for?

Answer:

HTTP status codes allow a server to communicate the result of processing a client request. Whenever there is a problem or error on the client side, the client error codes (400 series) are used. 401 is a client error code. It is used to specify unauthorised access. It indicates that the client needs to authenticate by specifying its credentials in order to be able to access a resource. If the client has already sent its credentials and still the 401 error occurs, then this indicates that the client has sent wrong credentials i.e. either an incorrect username or password.

20: What is the difference between the 4xx and 5xx codes?

Answer:

Both the 4xx and 5xx codes indicate that some error has occurred. However, the 4xx series are used to indicate client side errors. For example, 400 means that the user has sent a malformed URL, 401 means that the user is not authorised to access the request resource, etc. The 5xx series of codes are used to indicate that there is an error on the server side. Examples are 500 which means there was an error on the server while processing the request, 503 means that the server is unavailable as it is overloaded or down for maintenance, etc.

Chapter **3**

Java REST APIs and Implementations

21: What are the options available to develop RESTful services in Java?

Answer:

You can develop a RESTful service in Java in several ways:

a) You can use **servlets**. However, this approach requires you to write a lot of boilerplate code.

b) You can use **JAX-RS**. JAX-RS stands for Java API for RESTful Web Services. JAX-RS is a specification provided by Java. It is part of Java EE since Java 6.

c) **Spring REST** - Spring framework also provides rest capabilities as part of the Spring MVC component. This can also be used to develop a REST application.

22: Name some implementations of the JAX-RS API and explain.

Answer:

JAX-RS (Java API for RESTful Web Services) is a specification provided by Java EE for RESTful services. JAX-RS is just a specification; it does not provide an implementation. The following are some frameworks that implement the JAX-RS specification:

a) **Jersey** – Jersey is an open source framework that implements the JAX-RS specification. It also has additional capabilities to simplify the development of a REST service.

b) **RESTEasy** – RESTEasy is a JBOSS implementation of the JAX-RS framework.

c) **Apache CXF** – Apache CXF also implements the JAX-RS framework and can be used to build a REST application. In addition to JAX-RS, it also implements the JAX-WS specification and can be used to develop SOAP web services too.

23: What are the differences between Jersey and RESTEasy?

Answer:

Both Jersey and RESTEasy are implementations of the JAX-RS framework. However, there are several differences between the two:

a) Jersey is the reference implementation of the JAX-RS specification. RESTEasy is a JBOSS implementation of the JAX-RS specification.

b) Jersey provides a testing framework called Jersey Test Framework, which can be used to easily test the code. On the other hand, testing is not very easy with RESTEasy.

c) Jersey provides some ready Maven archetypes which can be used to start development quickly. RESTEasy, on the other hand, does not have Maven archetypes, so development has to be done from scratch.

d) RESTEasy supports caching easily via the `@Cache`, `@NoCache` annotations which sets the Cache headers accordingly in the response. Jersey does not have direct annotations that support caching.

e) RESTEasy provides support for GZip format easily. In Jersey, the GZip support is not so easy and has to be provided manually via Interceptors.

24: What is the difference between Jersey and Spring REST?

Answer:

Both the Jersey framework and Spring REST can be used to develop a REST service. However, there are a few differences between the two. Jersey is an implementation of the JAX-RS specification which is provided by Java EE for developing REST services. Spring REST, on the other hand, does not implement the JAX-RS specification; it provides its own REST implementations via the Spring MVC module. So, Spring REST is an alternative way of implementing a REST application. Another difference between the two is in the annotations used. The annotations used by JAX-RS in order to implement a REST service are different from the annotations used by Spring REST. For example, if a method in a class corresponds to an HTTP GET method, in JAX-RS you need to use the `@Get` annotation whereas in Spring you need to use the `@RequestMapping` or `@GetMapping` annotation.

25: What is Jackson?

Answer:

Jackson is a JSON library for Java. So, it supports automatically converting Java objects to JSON format and vice versa. Though it was initially created to support JSON, it supports other data formats too. It also implements the JAXB API and can be used to create XML output. The Jersey framework which is an implementation of the JAX-RS specification includes Jackson. So, it uses Jackson to convert Java objects to JSON format and vice versa. JSON created via Jackson contains embedded class information and so can create the complete object tree during the deserialization process.

26: What is JAXB?

Answer:

JAXB is an XML library for Java and supports automatically converting Java objects to XML format and vice versa. It stands for Java Architecture for XML binding. JAX-RS which is the Java specification for REST services uses JAXB when it needs to produce XML as the output data type. JAXB is just a specification and not an implementation. Jersey (which is a JAX-RS implementation), also implements the JAXB specification. Another implementation of JAXB is Moxy. JAXB is annotation based, so you just need to annotate your class with the appropriate annotations, and they will automatically be converted to XML format.

27: What is RESTlet?

Answer:

RESTlet is an open source framework that can be used to develop REST services in Java. It was the first RESTful framework available for developing REST services in Java and has been around since 2005. It is lightweight but can be extended easily due to its pluggable nature. It can be used to develop both REST servers and REST clients. It supports the HTTP protocol and XML and JSON data formats. It also provides an extension that implements the JAX-RS specification.

28: What are the steps in building a REST application that uses Jersey in Eclipse?

Answer:

The following steps need to be followed to create a REST application in Eclipse using JAX-RS and Jersey:

a) Ensure that your Eclipse uses Java 6 or higher

b) Create a new Dynamic web project

c) Add Jar files for Jersey framework in the WEB-INF lib folder

d) Write source code

e) In the web.xml file, specify the Jersey framework servlet in the servlet mapping

f) Setup Tomcat or the server of your choice in Eclipse

g) Deploy the application on the server (Right click on server, click on Add/Remove, Select application name and Click on Add)

h) Test application either using your browser or Postman

29: What are the advantages of Spring REST?

Answer:

The Spring framework supports building a REST application via its Spring MVC module. Spring's REST support does not implement the JAX-RS specification and it is an alternative way of developing a REST application. It offers several benefits:

a) Easy to integrate with other Spring modules like Spring Data JPA, Spring Security, etc.

b) SpringBoot (Which is built on top of Spring) helps to get a REST application up and running quickly.

c) It has dedicated annotations like `@RestController`, `@ResponseBody` which make development of a REST application easier.

d) Spring has inherent dependency injection features.

30: Can Jersey be used with Spring? If so, how?

Answer:

Jersey implements JAX-RS, which is the Java specification for REST services. Spring has its own REST support and does not implement the JAX-RS specification. But a Spring application can still be configured to use Jersey. For this, you need to follow the following steps:

a) Include the jersey-spring jar file. The maven dependency for this is as follows:

```
<dependency>
<groupId>org.glassfish.jersey.ext</groupId>
    <artifactId>jersey-spring4</artifactId>
    <version>2.26</version>
</dependency>
```

If you are using SpringBoot, it provides a starter for Jersey
which can be added via the following Maven dependency:

```
<!--
https://mvnrepository.com/artifact/org.springfr
amework.boot/spring-boot-starter-jersey -->
<dependency>
   groupId>org.springframework.boot</groupId>
   <artifactId>spring-boot-starter-
jersey</artifactId>
   <version>2.1.6.RELEASE</version>
</dependency>
```

b) Write code that uses JAX-RS annotations and not Spring
REST annotations.

This page is intentionally left blank

Chapter **4**

JAX–RS Basics

31: Which Java API is used for building a REST service?

Answer:

JAX-RS is a Java API that can be used for building a REST service. JAX-RS stands for Java API for RESTful Web Services (JAX-RS). It is part of the Java EE since Java 6, so does not need to be included separately. The latest version of JAX-RS is JAX-RS 2.0 and is part of Java EE 7. JAX-RS is just an API; it has some annotations that can be used to build a REST application. JAX-RS does not include an implementation. Jersey framework is the reference implementation of JAX-RS specification and implements JAX-RS 2.0. There are other implementations of JAX-RS like RESTEasy, etc.

32: What are the advantages of the JAX-RS specification?

Answer:

Before the JAX-RS API specification was developed, Servlets were used to create RESTful services. However, servlets require a lot of boilerplate code to be written. The JAX-RS specification helps to get rid of the boilerplate code. Using the JAX-RS specification, annotations can be applied to POJO classes. JAX-RS annotations can be used to associate URLs with methods in the code. It also has annotations that can be used to easily extract parameters from the HTTP request. It also has message body readers and writers which can automatically create data in the appropriate format (JSON or XML) from your Java objects. It also has exception mappers that can map application-specific exceptions to HTTP error codes.

33: Which JAX-RS annotations map to the HTTP methods?

Answer:

JAX-RS provides several annotations that map to various HTTP methods. These are as follows:

a) `@javax.ws.rs.GET` – maps to HTTP GET method

b) `@javax.ws.rs.PUT` – maps to HTTP PUT method

c) `@javax.ws.rs.POST` – maps to HTTP POST method

d) `@javax.ws.rs.DELETE` – maps to HTTP DELETE method

e) `@javax.ws.rs.HEAD` – maps to HTTP HEAD method

These annotations need to be specified on a JAX-RS method and indicate the HTTP method that the JAX-RS method maps to. So, when a client request comes in, the HTTP method in the client request will be matched to the method that has the appropriate annotation. If there is no annotation specified on a method, then it is assumed that it can cater to all HTTP methods.

34: Write a code sample that demonstrates a REST method that processes a GET request.

Answer:

The HTTP GET method is used to retrieve some information from a service. The following code demonstrates a REST method that processes a GET request:

```
@Path("getAllPerson")
@GET
@Produces("application/xml")
public Person getPerson(@PathParam("id") ) {
   System.out.println("Retrieving Person
objects:");
   // TODO Actual code
   }
```

Here, the `getAllPersonObjects` has the @GET annotation specified. It also has the @Produces with the media type as "application/xml" which indicates that this method produces an XML output. It accepts a single parameter as a path parameter which is the id of the Person object that is being queried. It returns a Person object. The Person class can be written as follows:

```
@XmlRootElement
public class Person {
   private String name;
  private int age;
//Getters and setters
  }
```

35: Write a sample code that demonstrates saving a custom object via REST.

Answer:

Suppose there is an Employee class as follows that needs to be saved:

```
public class Employee {
  private String name;
 private int id
//Getters and setters
}
```

You will need to write a method as follows on the server side:

```
@Path("saveemployee")
    @POST
    @Consumes("application/xml")
    public void saveEmployee(Employee
employee)
    {
  // write actual code
    }
```

So, this `saveEmployee` method maps to the `/saveemployee` path. Here, you will need to write the code for saving the object.

The client application needs to invoke this method via a POST request. It needs to send `Employee` data in XML format as follows:

```
<employee>
<name>Tom</name>
<id>30</id>
  </employee>
```

36: What is HTTP content negotiation and how is it handled by JAX-RS?

Answer:

In a REST application, the client and server applications communicate via the HTTP protocol. So, a client application can be written in any technology and the server application can be written in a different technology. However, different clients require data in different formats. So, depending on the technology that the client application is implemented in, it might require data in XML, JSON, HTML or plain text format. The HTTP protocol allows the client application to specify the format in which it wants the data via request headers. So, the client application can specify the format in which it wants the data, the data encoding strategy to be used, etc. This is known as HTTP content negotiation. In JAX-RS, the `@Produces` annotation can be used for content negotiation. So, the header information in the incoming request is matched to the method that has the same metadata specified in the `@Produces` annotation.

37: Which classes are available in JAX-RS framework that help to implement the HATEOAS principle?

Answer:

HATEOAS stands for Hypermedia As The Engine Of Application State. This principle allows embedding links to other resources or services in a REST response. Since HATEOAS needs to be implemented at the application level, JAX-RS does not have much support for it. However, JAX-RS does provide helper classes that can be used to build the URIs that are sent to the client application. One such helper class is the `UriBuilder` class. It has several methods that help you create a URI. Another class is the

`UriInfo` class that can be used to build relative URIs.

38: What is the use of the `@Produces` and `@Consumes` annotations?

Answer:

Both the `@Produces` and `@Consumes` annotation can be applied on a JAX-RS service class or method. The `@Produces` annotation defines the media type that a JAX-RS method is capable of producing while the `@Consumes` annotation is used to define the MIME type of the data that a JAX-RS service can accept. Both are used to narrow down a method that matches a client request. So, when a client request comes in, the headers in the request will be compared to the metadata specified in these annotations and only if there is a match, the corresponding method will be invoked. If the annotations are specified at the class level, the MIME type specified is applicable to all the methods in the class. If the annotations are specified at the method level, the method level annotations override the class level annotations. Some of the MIME types that can be specified with these annotations are text/plain, application/xml, application/json, etc.

39: How does client request matching work?

Answer:

When a client request comes in, the URI in the request is first matched with the value in the `@Path` annotation. A list of classes and methods that match the URI are shortlisted. The HTTP method in the incoming request (GET, POST, etc.) is then compared with the annotations specified on the matched methods (`@GET`, `@POST`, etc.) and the methods are further narrowed down. Finally, the content-type header in the client request is compared with the media type specified in the @Consumes annotation and the media type in the Accept header is compared with the media type specified in the @Produces annotation and the method that would service the client request is determined.

This page is intentionally left blank

Chapter **5**

JAX–RS Request Handling

40: What is the use of the @Path **annotation?**

Answer:

The @Path annotation can be used on any class or method in your code and identifies the URI to which the class or method will be mapped. So, you need to specify a URI with this annotation. If the annotation is specified at the class level, all the methods in the class will be mapped to the same URI. If the annotation is specified at the method level, the method level annotation overrides the class level annotation. A relative URI should be specified with the Path annotation. You can also specify an expression with the Path annotation which will be matched to the incoming URL.

41: Write a code sample that uses the `@PathParam` annotation.

Answer:

The `@PathParam` annotation is used to extract request parameters which are specified as part of the URL.

Consider the following code:

```
@Path("/person")
public class PersonService {
 public Person getPersonByFirstNameAndLastName
(@PathParam("firstname") String firstname,
    @PathParam("lastname") String lastname) {
  //TODO - code here
   }
}
```

Here, the `PersonService` has a method called `getPersonByFirstNameAndLastName` which returns a Person object based on the value passed in for first name and last name. Here, the `firstName` and `lastName` are passed in using the `@PathParam` annotation.

When a client application invokes this method, it can use the following URL:

```
/person/Mickey/Mouse
```

The values for the parameters `firstName` and `lastName` are passed as part of the URL. The value Mickey will be assigned to the `firstName` parameter and the value Mouse will be assigned to the `lastName` value parameter.

42: What is the difference between `@QueryParam` **and** `@PathParam`?

Answer:

Both `@QueryParam` and `@PathParam` are used to extract data from a URI. However, when `@PathParam` is used, the client application needs to send the parameters as part of the URI. Example is /url/param1/param2. When @QueryParam is used, the client application needs to send parameters as query parameters in the URL. A Query parameter is of the form name=value and must be specified after a "?" symbol at the end of the URL. Example is url?param1=value1&&param2=value2 Also, when a @PathParam is used, only the value of the parameter needs to be specified, whereas when @QueryParam is used, both parameter name and value need to be specified.

43: What is the use of the @HeaderParam annotation? Explain with an example.

Answer:

Sometimes, your application may need to find out header information in the incoming request. In such cases, the @HeaderParam annotation is useful. For example, the Accept-Language header specifies the language in which content is acceptable to a client application. Suppose, your REST service needs to find the value of this header in order to send appropriate data to the client, you can write code similar to the following:

```
@GET
@Produces("text/html")
public String process(@HeaderParam("Accept-
Language") String language) {
   return null; //TODO - write actual code here
}
```

Here, the process method has a single parameter called language; it has the @HeaderParam annotation specified, with the value "Accept-Language". So, the value of the "Accept-Language" header will be assigned to the "language" parameter.

44: Which annotation should be used to consolidate input parameters to a JAX-RS method? Explain with a code sample.

Answer:

The `@BeanParam` annotation can be used to consolidate parameters to a JAX-RS method. So, instead of sending several parameters to a method, you can send just a single parameter. Consider the following code:

```
public Response
savePerson(@QueryParam("firstName") String
personfirstName,
   @QueryParam("lastName") String personLastName,
@QueryParam("age") int personAge) {
   // TODO Actual code
}
```

Here, the `savePerson` method accepts three values as query parameters. This code does not look very clean. So, it can be re-written as follows:

```
public class PersonBean {
   @QueryParam("firstName")
 private String personFirstName;
   @QueryParam("lastName")
 private String personLastName;
   @QueryParam("age")
 private int age;
}
```

`PersonBean` is a POJO class that has fields corresponding to the query parameters. Each field in the `PersonBean` class has appropriate annotations. The `savePerson` method can be re-written as follows:

```
public Response savePerson(@BeanParam
PersonBean personBean) {
   // TODO Actual code
}
```

So compared to the earlier code, this code is much cleaner.

45: What is the `@CookieParam` annotation used for?

Answer:

Cookies are generally used in web applications. A server can store some information in a cookie and send it to a client along with the response. The next time the client makes a request to the server, it can send the cookie and the server can identify the client based on the value in the cookie. Cookies can also be used in a JAX-RS service, so a service method can also send a cookie to a client application and the client application can send it back to the server in a subsequent request. The `@CookieParam` annotation can be used in such scenarios to retrieve the cookie information sent by a client application.

46: What is the use of the `@DefaultValue` annotation?

Answer:

The `@DefaultValue` annotation can be used to specify a default value for a JAX-RS method parameter. Sometimes, the parameter to a JAX-RS method may be optional, so a client application may not specify a value. In such scenarios, JAX-RS uses a null or zero value for the missing parameter. However, using a null or zero value as the default may affect the business logic and you may need to specify a default value that is suited for your application. In such cases, the `@DefaultValue` annotation is useful. Along with the annotation, you also need to specify a value that should be used as default in case the client application does not send a value. If a client application sends a value for the parameter, the value sent by the client application will be used, otherwise, the default value specified will be used.

47: How are matrix parameters different from query parameters?

Answer:

Both matrix and query parameters are parameters which can be specified as name value pairs. However, there are some differences between the two:

a) Query parameters occur at the end of the URL, matrix parameters occur in between the URL.

b) Query parameters are followed after the "?" sign, matrix parameters are specified after the ";" sign.

c) Matrix parameters are related to part of a URL, query parameters are related to the full URL.

Chapter **6**

JAX-RS Response Handling

48: Write a code sample that demonstrates a REST method that returns data in plain text format.

Answer:

The following code sample demonstrates a REST method that returns data in plain text format:

```
@GET
 @Produces("text/plain")
 public String getGreeting() {
   return "Hello World!";
 }
```

Here, the getGreeting method has the @Produces annotation specified. It has the value "text/plain" which indicates that the method returns plain text data. The return type of the method is String. So, the value "Hello World" is returned by the method. The @Get annotation is specified which indicates that this method processes an HTTP GET request

49: Explain the `javax.ws.rs.core.Response` **class and what it is used for.**

Answer:

The `javax.ws.rs.core.Response` is a class that can be used to control the response sent back to the client. Sometimes, you may want to customize the response sent by a method, and in such cases you can have the method return a `javax.ws.rs.core.Response` object instead of sending the actual entity that your method may return. The `Response` class has several methods that can be used to set the response status, data in the response, response headers, etc. `Response` objects cannot be created directly. They can only be created via `ResponseBuilder` instances. The client application can use the `Response` object to retrieve the information sent by the REST service.

50: What is the `ResponseBuilder` **class? Explain with a code sample.**

Answer:

The `ResponseBuilder` is a factory class that can be used to create `Response` objects. It is a nested class within the `Response` class. `Response` objects cannot be created directly; they can be created only via a `ResponseBuilder`. There are static methods on the `Response` class that return a `ResponseBuilder` instance. The `ResponseBuilder` has a method called build which in turn creates and returns a Response instance. For example, consider the following code:

```
ResponseBuilder builder = Response.status(400);
Response response = builder.build();
```

Here, the `Response.status` method is used which creates a `ResponseBuilder` corresponding to the status 400 which means that a wrong URL is sent by the client application. The `ResponseBuilder.build()` method is then invoked which creates and returns a `Response` instance with status 400.

51: What is the use of the `Response.created` method?

Answer:

The `Response.created` is a static method on the `Response` class. This method is generally used to create a `Response` when a client application sends a POST or PUT request to indicate to the client application that a resource is created successfully. It accepts a URI as a parameter which is the URI of the newly created resource. It returns a `ResponseBuilder` instance corresponding to status code 201. The following code sample demonstrates this:

```
ResponseBuilder builder = Response.created();
Response response = builder.build();
```

52: How can you create a `Response` object with a particular status code?

Answer:

There are several methods on the `Response` class that let you create a `Response` object with a particular status code:

a) `Response.status(int status)` – This accepts an integer status code and returns a `ResponseBuilder` instance.

b) `Response.status(Response.status status)` – This accepts an `enum` value of the `Response.Status` type and returns a `ResponseBuilder` instance.

c) `Response.status(Response.StatusType status)` – This accepts a value of the `Response.StatusType` and returns a `ResponseBuilder` instance.

In addition, there are several methods on the `Response` class that create `ResponseBuilder` instances with particular status codes. For example, the `Response.ok` creates a `ResponseBuilder` with the code as 200, the `Response.notModified` creates a `ResponseBuilder` with the code as 304.

53: What is the use of the `Response.readEntity` method? Explain with a code sample.

Answer:

The `Response.readEntity` method can be used by a client application to retrieve a Java object sent by a server. It accepts as parameter, a `Class` instance, and maps the information into the response to an object of the specified class. If the data in the response cannot be converted to an object of the class, it throws an exception. The following code demonstrates this:

```
Person person = response.readEntity(Person.class);
```

Here, the `response.readEntity` is used to retrieve a `Person` object from the response stream which is assigned to the variable "person".

54: What is the difference between `getHeaderString` and `getStringHeaders` method?

Answer:

Both the `getHeaderString` and `getStringHeaders` are

methods on the Response class and can be used by a client application to retrieve header information. However, there are some differences between the two. The getHeaderString returns a single String value that corresponds to all the headers. So, all the header names and values are concatenated to produce a single String value. The getStringHeaders, on the other hand, returns a MultiValuedMap. MultiValuedMap is an interface like the java.util.Map interface and can be used to store key value pairs. So, the MultiValuedMap has each header name and its value.

55: Write a code sample that demonstrates the @Produces **annotation.**

Answer:

The @Produces annotation is used to specify the MIME type of data that a JAX-RS service is capable of producing and is useful in narrowing down a client request. The following code snippet demonstrates the @Produces annotation:

```
@GET
@Produces("text/plain")
public String getGreeting() {
  return "Hello World!";
}
```

Here, the getGreeting method is annotated with @Produces annotation. The value text/plain is specified to indicate that it produces a text based output. Other values like application/xml, or application/json can be specified to indicate that the method produces an XML or JSON output.

56: Write a code sample that demonstrates the `@Consumes` annotation.

Answer:

The `@Consumes` annotation is used to specify the MIME type of the data that a JAX-RS service can accept. The following code snippet demonstrates the `@Consumes` annotation:

```
@XmlRootElement
public class Person {
 private String name;
 private int age;
//Getters and setters
}
```

This is a `Person` class with 2 fields for `name` and `age`.

```
 @Path("consumedemo")
  @POST
  @Consumes("application/xml")
  public void processPerson(Person person)
  {
    System.out.println("Processing Person
request:");
    System.out.println(" Name :
"+person.getName());
    System.out.println(" Age : "+person.getAge());
  }
```

The `processPerson` method has the `@Consumes` annotation with the media type as XML. So, you need to send a `Person` object in XML format to this method. You can test this method via Postman using the following XML data:

```
<person>
<name>Bill</name>
<age>20</age>
 </person>
```

In addition to `application/xml`, the values

`application/json, plain/text` etc. can be used to specify that the method accepts a JSON or text type data.

57: What is the use of the `Response.ok` method?

Answer:

The `Response.ok` method is used to create an HTTP response with status as 200 which means that the request was processed successfully. There are three overloaded versions of this method as follows:

a) `Response.ok()` – This creates a `ResponseBuilder` with 200 OK status.

b) `Response.ok(Object entity)` – This creates a `ResponseBuilder` with 200 OK status and includes the specified object in the response.

c) `Response.ok(Object entity, MediaType type)` – This creates a `ResponseBuilder` with 200 OK status and includes the specified object in the response in the format specified by the `MediaType` parameter (XML, JSON, etc.).

This page is intentionally left blank

Chapter **7**

JAX–RS Exception Handling

58: How does exception handling work in a REST application?

Answer:

A REST method can report an error to a client either via an HTTP response code or by throwing an exception. In case a REST application throws an exception, it also needs to define an exception mapper. An exception mapper is nothing but a class that converts the exception to the appropriate HTTP status code. So, when an exception is thrown, the exception is handled by the JAX-RS runtime via the exception mapper. If no mapper is provided, the exception is propagated and handled by the servlet container. A REST method can throw either a checked or an unchecked exception.

59: What is the use of javax.ws.rs.WebApplicationException?

Answer:

`javax.ws.rs.WebApplicationException` is an in-built checked exception provided by JAX-RS. It includes a status code and `Response` object. Since this is an in-built exception, the application code does not need to provide an exception mapper. At the time of throwing this exception, the application code can initialize the `WebApplicationException` with an appropriate status code or `Response` object. Once the exception is thrown, JAX-RS catches the exception and uses the `Response` object and status code within the exception to send an appropriate HTTP response to the client. If there is no status code or `Response` object provided by the application code, the `WebApplicationException` sends status code of 500 which means "Internal Server Error" to the client.

60: Write a code sample that demonstrates an `ExceptionMapper` for a custom exception.

Answer:

The following code demonstrates a custom exception mapper:

```
@Provider
public class ApplicationExceptionMapper implements
ExceptionMapper<ApplicationException>{
 @Override
 public Response toResponse(ApplicationException
ex) {
  return
Response.status(Response.Status.INTERNAL_SERVER_ERR
OR).build();
  }
}
```

This is an `ExceptionMapper` for a custom exception called

`ApplicationException`. It has the `@Provider` annotation. The `ApplicationExceptionMapper` class implements the `ExceptionMapper` interface and overrides the `toResponse` method. In this method, you can place the correct HTTP Status code. In this case, the HTTP status code for Internal Server Error i.e. code 500 is used. So, this code will be sent to the client when the `ApplicationException` occurs.

61: What is the `ForbiddenException`?

Answer:

JAX-RS provides an in-built exception hierarchy to handle various error conditions corresponding to various HTTP status codes. So, if your application can cause any of these errors, you need not create a custom exception, you can use one of these in-built exceptions. At the top of the exception hierarchy is the `WebApplicationException`. This has various sub-classes, one such being the `ForbiddenException`. The `ForbiddenException` corresponds to HTTP status code 403 and indicates that the client application is not permitted to access the requested resource.

62: How can you create a `WebApplicationException` instance?

Answer:

`javax.ws.rs.WebApplicationException` is an in-built checked exception provided by JAX-RS. There are several ways in which it can be created:

a) **Using `Response` object –**
   `WebApplicationException(Response response)`

b) **Using status code** – `WebApplicationException(int status)`

c) **Using error message** – `WebApplicationException(String message)`

d) **Using** `Response` **status** – `WebApplicationException(Response.Status status)`

e) **Using** `Throwable` **instance** – `WebApplicationException(Throwable cause)`

f) **Using** `Throwable` **instance and status** – `WebApplicationException(Throwable cause, int status)`

g) **Using** `Throwable` **instance and** `Response` – `WebApplicationException(Throwable cause, Response response)`

h) **Using** `Throwable` **instance and error message** – `WebApplicationException(String message, Throwable cause)`

i) **Using error message and** `Response` – `WebApplicationException(String message, Response response)`

63: Explain the `NotFoundException` **and write a sample code that throws this exception.**

Answer:

The `NotFoundException` is an in-built exception that can be thrown when a resource requested by a client application is not found. It corresponds to the status code 404. It is a sub-class of the `WebApplicationException` class. The following code demonstrates this:

```
@GET
@Path("{/person/")
@Produces("application/xml")
public Person getPerson(@PathParam("id") int id) {
Person person = findPerson(id);
if (person == null) {
throw new NotFoundException());
}
return person;
}
}
```

The getPerson method retrieves a Person object corresponding to the specified id. If there is no person object, the NotFoundException is thrown. This will cause a Response object with the status code 404 to be sent to the client.

64: Which exception will be thrown when there is no JAX-RS method that produces the media type specified in the accept request header?

Answer:

When there is no JAX-RS method that produces the media type specified in the accept request header, the NotAcceptableException is thrown. This corresponds to the 406 status code. The JAX-RS matches the media type in the accept request header with the media type specified in the @Produces annotation on each method and if there is no match, this exception will be thrown. If the @Produces annotation is specified on any method, it means that the method can produce all types of data, so no exception will be thrown. This exception may also be explicitly thrown by the application code.

This page is intentionally left blank

Chapter **8**

JAX–RS Client

65: What are the ways in which you can create a REST client application?

Answer:

There are several ways in which you can create a client application that queries a REST service. You can use Java's built-in HTTP client library which consists the `java.net.URL` and `java.net.HttpURLConnection` classes. JAX-RS implementations like Jersey also provide a client API which can be used. The downside to using Jersey client API or any other JAX-RS implementation specific API is that the client code becomes tied down to the JAX-RS implementation that you are using, so it will not possible to use some other JAX-RS implementation easily. JAX-RS 2.0 also provides a client API which was introduced to solve all these issues. JAX-RS client API is implemented by all the major JAX-RS vendors like Jersey and RESTEasy and so any implementation can be used. The advantage of using the JAX-RS API as against the vendor specified API is that the vendor can easily be changed without changing the code.

66: What is the use of the `javax.ws.rs.client.ClientBuilder` **interface?**

Answer:

The `javax.ws.rs.client.ClientBuilder` is the starting point of the JAX-RS 2.0 Client API.

It has static methods that can be used to create instances of the `javax.ws.rs.client.Client` classes. The `ClientBuilder.newClient()` method is most commonly used for creating a `Client` instance.

There is a `ClientBuilder.newBuilder` method that can be used to create a customized `ClientBuilder` instance. It implements the `Configurable` interface and so methods like `register` from the `Configurable` interface can be used to register a client request/response filter, etc.

67: What is the use of the `javax.ws.rs.client.Client` **interface?**

Answer:

The `javax.ws.rs.client.Client` interface is part of the JAX-RS client API. It is used while writing client code for a JAX-RS application. It is responsible for managing the client side communication. There is a class called `ClientBuilder` which can be used to create a `Client` instance. Once a `Client` instance is obtained, you can use it to connect to the service URI and query the server. The `javax.ws.rs.client.Client` is a heavyweight and expensive class to create. So very few instances should be created of this class and they should be reused as and when possible.

68: Explain the purpose of the `WebTarget` **interface.**

Answer:

The `WebTarget` interface can be used to represent the URI that you want the client application to invoke. There are several `target()` methods available on the `javax.ws.rs.client.Client` class that can be used to create a `WebTarget` instance. `WebTarget` also has several additional methods that can be used to extend the URI that it was originally constructed with. So, for example, the path method can be used to create a new `WebTarget` instance with the specified path. It also has methods that can be used to dynamically specify values for parameters. For example, the `resolveTemplate` method can be used to replace a path variable with a particular value.

69: How can you use `WebTarget` **to resolve a path parameter? Explain with a code sample.**

Answer:

The `WebTarget` interface can be used to represent the URI that you want the client application to invoke. `WebTarget` also has several methods that can be used to dynamically specify values for parameters. The following code demonstrates this:

```
 WebTarget target =
client.target("http://personapp.com/persons/{id}")
    .resolveTemplate("id", "45");
```

Here, the `client.target` method is used to create a

`WebTarget` corresponding to the
`http://personapp.com/persons/{id}` URI. This URI has
id as a path parameter. The `resolveTemplate` method is also
invoked on the target object. This method accepts two parameters
corresponding to the parameter name and parameter value. Here,
the value 45 is passed corresponding to the id parameter, so this
value will be used in the URI when the REST service is invoked.

70: What are the steps in creating an `Invocation.Builder` **to
invoke a REST service?**

Answer:

A `WebTarget` instance can be used to build an
`Invocation.Builder` instance. You need to follow the
following steps to invoke the REST service:

a) You first need to set the request headers. The
    `Invocation.Builder` has several methods for setting
    request headers. So, for example, the `acceptLanguage`
    can be used to specify the accept language request header,
    the `acceptEncoding` method can be used to set the accept
    encoding request header, etc.

b) After setting the request headers, you can invoke the
    appropriate HTTP methods. So, there are methods like GET,
    POST, etc. available on the `Invocation.Builder`
    interface which correspond to HTTP methods. You can
    invoke the appropriate method. This returns a Response
    instance.

71: What is the use of the `WebTarget.queryParam` **method?**
Explain with a code sample.

Answer:

The `WebTarget` interface can be used to represent the URI that you want the client application to invoke. It has several methods that can be used to dynamically specify values for parameters. One such method is the `queryParam` method. It can be used to specify a query parameter. It accepts two parameters, the query parameter name and query parameter value. For example, consider the following code:

```
WebTarget target =
client.target("http://personapp.com/persons")
   .queryParam("id", "45");
```

This will add a query parameter called id with the value 45 to the URI specified in the `client.target` method. So, this request will resolve to the following URL:

```
http://personapp.com/persons?id=45
```

72: Explain the `Invocation.Builder` **interface.**

Answer:

`Invocation` is an interface that encapsulates a request by a client to invoke a REST service. The `Invocation` interface represents a request that has been prepared and is ready for execution. It has a method called `invoke` which actually invokes the REST service and obtains a `Response` instance. It has a nested interface called `Builder`. The `Builder` interface has methods for preparing the client request invocation. So, it has methods for setting the request headers, etc. Once the request has been prepared by the `Invocation.Builder`, the `Invocation.invoke` method can be used to submit it.

73: Write a sample code that demonstrates how to create a client application that queries a REST service.

Answer:

The following code demonstrates a JAX-RS client:

```
public class JaxRsClientDemo {
static String URI =
"http://localhost:8080/RestJAXRSJerseyDemo/lea
rnjava/myservice";
  public static void main(String args[]) {
  Client client = ClientBuilder.newClient();
  WebTarget target = client.target(URI);
  Invocation.Builder invocationBuilder =
target.request();
  Response response = invocationBuilder.get();
  String responseStr =
response.readEntity(String.class);
  System.out.println("Server
Response:"+responseStr);
  }
```

This code does the following:

a) Creates `Client` instance using the `ClientBuilder.newClient` factory method

b) Creates a `WebTarget` using the `client.target` method and the URI to be used, in this case `"http://localhost:8080/RestJAXRSJerseyDemo/learnjava/myservice`

c) Creates an `Invocation.Builder` instance using the `target.request()` method

d) Creates a `Response` object using the `invocationBuilder.get()`

e) Read the data sent by the server via the `response.getEntity` method

Chapter 9

JAX–RS Filters

74: What are the types of filters that can be specified in a REST application?

Answer:

There are basically two types of filters that can be used in a REST application, server side and client side. Server side filters are applied on the server side to the client request. There are two types of server side filters, request filters and response filters. A request filter is applied to a request before it is sent to the client application. A response filter is applied to the server's response before it is sent to the client. The client side filters are applied on the client side. Client side filters are again classified into request and response filters. The request filters are applied to the client's request before it is sent to the server and the response filters are applied to the server's response before it is sent to the client.

75: What is the use of a server side or client side filter?

Answer:

Server side filters help in modifying a request from a client before it is sent to the server or a response from the server before it is sent to client. Client side filters help in modifying a client request before it is sent to the server or the server's response before it is sent to the client. So basically, you can place any common code that needs to be executed on all requests/responses in the filter. Normally, any code that is protocol related or not related to your business logic can be placed in a filter. Filters can also be used to write some extensions to the JAX-RS API.

76: Explain the types of server side filters.

Answer:

There are two different types of server side filters, request filters and response filters. A request filter is basically just some code that needs to be executed before a client request is sent to a JAX-RS method. It may modify the client request is some ways like adding/removing a header, etc. A request filter may be applied before the request is matched to a method or after a request is matched to a method. A response filter is some code that needs to be executed to modify the server's response before it is sent to the client application. Both request and response filters can be applied to all JAX-RS methods or they can be limited to only specific methods.

77: What are the @PreMatching **and** @PostMatching **annotations used for?**

Answer:

ContainerRequestFilter is an interface that needs to be implemented by any class that needs to provide a server side request filter. It has a single method called filter. Here, the filtering code that needs to be executed before sending request to the JAX-RS service method needs to be specified. The @PreMatching and @PostMatching annotations can be applied to the ContainerRequestFilter. The @PreMatching annotation simply specifies that the code within the filter method should be executed before the request is mapped to a JAX-RS method and the @PostMatching annotation specifies that the code within the filter method should be executed after the request is matched to a JAX-RS method.

78: What is the ContainerResponseFilter **interface?**

Answer:

ContainerResponseFilter is an interface that needs to be implemented by any class that needs to provide a server side response filter. It can be used to modify the response before it is sent to the client. It has a filter method where the code that needs to be executed before the response is sent to the client application needs to be specified.

The filter method accepts two parameters, ContainerRequestContext and ContainerResponseContext.

The ContainerRequestContext can be used to access information about the request. It can be used to modify the response as required before it is sent to the client. So, you can modify the response header or set some additional information in the response.

79: Write a code sample that demonstrates how the `ContainerRequestFilter` **can be used to filter the incoming request.**

Answer:

The `ContainerRequestFilter` can be used to implement a server side request filter. So, when a client application sends a request, it can be filtered before being sent to the actual JAX-RS service method. The following code demonstrates this:

```
@PreMatching
@Provider
public class MyRequestFilter implements
ContainerRequestFilter {
  public void
filter(ContainerRequestContext
containerRequest) throws IOException {
    if
    (containerRequest.getMethod().equals("DELETE"))
        containerRequest.abortWith(Response.status
        (Response.Status.FORBIDDEN).build());
  }
}
```

The `MyRequestFilter` class provides a request filter by implementing the `ContainerRequestFilter` interface. The filter method is used to prevent the client application from sending an HTTP DELETE method. So, if the HTTP method is DELETE, a FORBIDDEN response is sent to the client. Here, the `@PreMatching` annotation is specified on the class, this indicates that the filter method will be executed before the request is mapped to the service method.

80: What is the use of the `ContainerRequestContext` **interface?**

Answer:

The `ContainerRequestContext` instance is accepted as a parameter by the `filter` method in the `ContainerRequestFilter` and `ContainerResponseFilter` interfaces. It can be used to obtain information about the request like HTTP method, request headers, etc. which can then be used in the `filter` method. It has getter methods like `getAcceptableLanguages`, `getAcceptableMediaTypes` that allow retrieving information from the request. It also has setter methods that can be used to modify the request. It also has a method called `abortWith` which can be used to terminate the filter chain and send a Response to the client.

81: Write a code sample that demonstrates the `ContainerResponseFilter` **interface.**

Answer:

The `ContainerResponseFilter` is used to implement a response filter which modifies the response before it is sent to the client. The following code demonstrates this:

```
@Provider
public class MyResponseFilter implements
ContainerResponseFilter {
  public void filter(ContainerRequestContext
req, ContainerResponseContext res) throws
IOException {
    if (req.getMethod().equals("POST")) {
    res.getHeaders().add("MyHeader",
"MyHeaderValue");
```

```
    }
   }
 }
```

Here, the `MyResponseFilter` class implements the `ContainerResponseFilter`. The filter method accepts `ContainerRequestContext` and `ContainerResponseContext` instances as arguments. The code obtains the HTTP method from the `ContainerRequestContext` and checks if it is a POST request. If so, it adds a custom header called `MyHeader` with the value `MyHeaderValue` to the response.

82: Explain the `ClientRequestFilter` interface with a code sample.

Answer:

The `ClientRequestFilter` is an interface that must be implemented by any class that wants to create a request filter on the client side. A client side request filter filters a client request before it is sent to the REST service. `ClientRequestFilter` has a single method called filter. This is invoked before the client's request is sent to the REST service. The following code demonstrates this:

```
public class MyClientFilter implements
ClientRequestFilter{
  public void filter(ClientRequestContext
  clientRequestContext) throws IOException {
    clientRequestContext.getHeaders().add("Conte
    nt-Type", "application/json;");
  }
}
```

Here, the `MyClientFilter` class implements a client filter. In the filter method, the content-type request header is added with the value as application/json. So basically, before the client request is sent to the rest service, this content type is set in the request to indicate to the REST service that the client can understand only JSON content type.

83: Write a code sample that demonstrates how a client side response filter should be implemented.

Answer:

A client side response filter filters the response sent by a JAX-RS service before sending it to the client application. The ClientResponseFilter interface must be implemented by any class that wants to create a response filter on the client side. ClientResponseFilter has a method called filter which must be overridden with the filtering code. The following code demonstrates this:

```
public class MyClientResponseFilter implements
ClientResponseFilter{
  public void filter(ClientRequestContext arg0,
  ClientResponseContext arg1) throws
  IOException {
    // TODO Auto-generated method stub
  }
}
```

Here, MyClientResponseFilter implements the ClientResponseFilter interface. The filter method should have the actual filtering logic.

Also, the client code needs to be written as follows:

```
ClientBuilder builder =
ClientBuilder.newBuilder();
Client client = builder.register(new
```

```
MyClientResponseFilter()).build();
```

So here, instead of using the `ClientBuilder.newClient` method, the `ClientBuilder.newBuilder` method is invoked to obtain a `ClientBuilder` instance. The register method is then invoked on the `ClientBuilder` with an instance of `MyClientResponseFilter`, followed by the build method. This returns a `Client` instance.

Chapter **10**

JAX–RS Asynchronous Processing

84: How does asynchronous request processing work in JAX-RS? Explain the important classes that are used in asynchronous processing.

Answer:

JAX-RS supports asynchronous client processing. So, a client application can create several HTTP requests and send them to the REST server without waiting for a response. The client application can obtain a response either by polling the server or registering a callback that will notify the client once the response is available. This allows the client application to send separate parallel requests. The `Invocation.Builder` class has a method called `async`, this should be used in case the client wishes to make an asynchronous call. The `Invocation.Builder.async`

method returns `javax.ws.rs.client.AsyncInvoker`
instance. This has various methods that can be used to actually
make the HTTP call asynchronously. The methods on the
`AsyncInvoker` interface return a Future instance which can be
used to obtain the response.

**85: Explain the `AsyncInvoker` interface and write a code
sample that uses this interface to invoke a GET method
asynchronously.**

Answer:

The `AsyncInvoker` interface can be used by a JAX-RS client to
asynchronously invoke REST methods on the server. The
`Invocation.Builder` has a method called async, this returns
an instance of the `AsyncInvoker`. The `AsyncInvoker` has
various methods like get, post, delete, etc. which can be used to
invoke the appropriate HTTP method. The methods on the
`AsyncInvoker` interface return a Future instance which can be
used to obtain the response. The following code demonstrates
invoking a GET method asynchronously:

```
Client client = ClientBuilder.newClient();
WebTarget target = client.target(URI);
Invocation.Builder invocationBuilder =
target.request();
AsyncInvoker invoker =
invocationBuilder.async();
Future<Response> future = invoker.get();
```

86: How can a JAX-RS client that sends an asynchronous request process the response via a Callback?

Answer:

There is an interface called `InvocationCallBack`. This interface must be implemented by a class in order to provide a callback. This has two methods as follows:

  a) `Completed` – This is invoked when the server has completed processing the request successfully.

  b) `failed` – This is invoked when the server has failed processing the request.

The `AsyncInvoker` has an overloaded version of the GET method which accepts a Callback instance. So, when this GET method is invoked, the Callback is registered. The client does not need to poll the Future object that is returned; the Callback methods (completed or failed) will be invoked automatically once the request is completed.

87: Explain the differences between using the polling approach and callback approach.

Answer:

Both polling and callback method are ways in which a client application can obtain a response from an asynchronous HTTP call. When a polling implementation is used, you need to invoke the Future.get method to obtain the response. This is a blocking call that waits till a response is obtained. On the other hand, in the callback approach, the methods in the callback interface are invoked automatically when the HTTP method completes. The polling approach should generally be used when the client application wants to know when each asynchronous HTTP request has completed, and you need to perform some action after each HTTP request completes. The callback approach on the other hand should be used when the client application need not know when each HTTP method has completed.

88: What is the advantage of asynchronous server side processing?

Answer:

The nature of HTTP is that each client request is handled by a separate thread on the server side. However, there are scenarios where a client application may continuously poll a server method for some data. An example could be a weather service, which continuously sends the current temperature to the client. In such scenarios, creating a separate thread per client request can be expensive. To solve this issue, asynchronous server side processing was introduced. In this approach, you can suspend the calling thread and have a separate thread other than the calling thread to send a response to the client. This reduces the overhead of one thread per client model. Instead a smaller number of threads can be created to send data to polling clients.

89: How can asynchronous processing be applied on the server side?

Answer:

An interface called `AsyncResponse` is present which can be used to implement server side asynchronous processing. It has to be passed as a parameter to a method that provides a JAX-RS service. The `@Suspended` annotation should be used with the `AsyncResponse` instance that is passed in to the JAX-RS method. Also, a new Thread has to be created in the JAX-RS service method and the code needs to be placed there. This causes the JAX-RS method to create a new thread and do the processing in this thread. The `AsyncResponse.resume` method needs to be invoked from the thread to send the response to the client.

This page is intentionally left blank

Chapter **11**

JAX–RS Security

90: How can you enforce authentication and authorization for a JAX-RS method?

Answer:

Authentication simply means that a user or client application with correct credentials should be able to access the JAX-RS method. Authorisation means that even after authentication is successful, the user or client application needs to have the correct permissions or roles in order to be able to access the service. JAX-RS makes use of the security features provided by servlets and Java EE for authentication and authorization, it has an API to do this. In order to enable authentication and authorization for a JAX-RS method, you need to set up authentication information in the deployment descriptor (web.xml) and set up authorization in web.xml or enable it via annotations.

91: What are the steps in setting up authentication and authorization information in web.xml?

Answer:

In order to enable authentication and authorization for a JAX-RS method, you need to make the following changes to the deployment descriptor (web.xml):

a) Specify the `<login-config>` xml element where you specify the authentication method (basic, digest or client certification).

b) Setup the URL pattern that you want to secure via the `<security-constraint><url-pattern>` element.

c) Specify the HTTP method (GET, POST, etc.) that you want to secure via the `<security-constraint><http-method>`. If no method is specified, then all HTTP methods will be secured.

d) Specify the roles that are allowed to access the URL pattern via the `<security-constraint><auth-constraint><role-name>` element.

e) Specify role name in the `<security-role>` element.

92: What are the different ways of setting up authorization in a JAX-RS application? Explain which is a better way to setup authorization.

Answer:

There are two ways in which you can setup authorization in a JAX-RS application:

a) **Via the web.xml** – In this approach, you can configure the roles via the `<security-role>` and `<auth-constraint>` XML elements.

b) **Using annotations** – In this approach, you can annotate your JAX-RS service class or methods by specifying the appropriate annotations like @RolesAllowed, @PermitAll, etc.

Configuring the authorization information is generally a job for administrators and not developers. So, if it is done using annotations, the administrators will need to have access to the code and the code will need to be compiled each time some roles are changed. If authorization is done via XML, admins can easily change role information. So, setting up the authorization information in the web.xml is a better approach.

93: What is the use of the @RolesAllowed **annotation?**

Answer:

The way authorization works is that users are assigned to one or more roles and permissions are given based on roles, that is only certain roles are able to access certain methods. The @RolesAllowed annotation specifies a list of roles that are allowed to access a JAX-RS method. It can be specified at the class or method level in a JAX-RS service. If specified at the class level, it is applicable to all methods in the class. If it is specified at a method level, it is applicable to only the particular method. If it is specified at both the class and method level, the method level annotation overrides the class level annotation.

94: What is the use of the javax.ws.rs.core.SecurityContext **interface?**

Answer:

The javax.ws.rs.core.SecurityContext interface can be used by a JAX-RS application to collect security information about a secured JAX-RS request. A JAX-RS method can be passed the `SecurityContext` as a parameter by specifying the `@Context` annotation. Once a JAX-RS method receives the `SecurityContext` instance, it can access security information about the request via methods on the `SecurityContext` interface. For example, the `isSecure` method can be used to check if the request is secured, the `isUserInRole` method can be used to determine the role that a user is in, the `getAuthenticationScheme` method can be used to determine the HTTP authentication method used, etc.

Chapter **12**

JAX–RS Miscellaneous

95: What is the use of the `Link` and `Link.Builder` classes?

Answer:

The `Link` and `Link.Builder` classes can be used to include links in the JAX-RS response in order to achieve the HATEOAS principle. The `Link` class represents the actual link. In addition to the URI, it also contains information like the type of link, etc. The `Link` class has a method called `getUri` which refers to the actual URI. The `Link.Builder` class can be used to create a Link instance. It has various methods that can be used to build URIs from a String value, from a URI, etc.

96: How does JAX-RS support caching?

Answer:

HTTP supports a header called Cache-Control, this can be used to send caching information to a client. The Cache-Control header has a number of properties which can be used to send information like whether or not to cache data, how long the client can store the cache information, etc. There is a class called `javax.ws.rs.core.CacheControl` provided by JAX-RS. This can be used to set caching information in the Cache-Control header. It has various methods which can be used to set properties on the Cache-Control header. There is a method called `cacheControl` on the `ResponseBuilder` class which can be used to set the `CacheControl` instance in the Response object.

97: What is the use of the `javax.ws.rs.core.EntityTag` **class?**

Answer:

HTTP supports revalidation which is the process in which a client application asks a server if the data that it holds in the cache is still valid. When the server sends the data to the client the first time, it sends the Last-Modified header which has the timestamp of when the data was sent to the client. It also sends a header called `ETag` which represents the version of the data sent to the client. When the client requests information from the server the next time, it can perform a conditional GET by sending this Last-Modified header and the `ETag` header back to the server and requesting the server to send data only if the resource has been modified. The sever matches the `ETag` information sent by the client with the current `ETag` value and sends the data only if the `ETag`s are different which indicate that the data has been updated. The `javax.ws.rs.core.EntityTag` that represents the `ETag` header. It has various methods for setting and retrieving the `ETag` value.

98: How can you use Java's built in HTTP client library to connect to a REST service?

Answer:

Java's built in HTTP client library consists of two main classes which can be used to connect to a REST service, the java.net.URL and `java.net.HttpURLConnection`. The following code demonstrates how these classes can be used to obtain data from a JAX-RS service:

```
URL url = new URL(URI);
    HttpURLConnection connection =
(HttpURLConnection) url.openConnection();
    connection.setRequestMethod("GET");
    connection.setRequestProperty("Accept",
"text/plain");
    if (connection.getResponseCode() == 200) {
    System.out.println("Success!!");
    BufferedReader reader = new
BufferedReader(new
InputStreamReader(con.getInputStream()));
    String line = reader.readLine();
    while (line != null) {
     System.out.println(line);
     line = reader.readLine();
    }
    con.disconnect();
    }
```

First a new URL instance is created using the URI of the REST service and an `HttpURLConnection` is obtained using the URL instance. The HTTP method that is GET and the data type i.e. text/plain is then set on the connection object. The response code is checked and if it is 200, the actual data is read via a `BufferedReader`.

99: What are interceptors in the context of a JAX-RS application?

Answer:

Just like filters, Interceptors are also classes that act on and modify the server or client request or response. However, filters act on and modify the headers in the request/response. Interceptors on the other hand, act on and modify the request or response body. So, for example, suppose you want to compress the data in a request or response, you can use an interceptor to write the compression logic. Interceptors can be created on the client as well as server side. There are two interfaces provided by JAX-RS, `ReaderInterceptor` and `WriterInterceptor`. These need to be implemented by any class that needs to provide an interceptor.

100: What is the use of the `javax.ws.rs.core.Request` class?

Answer:

The `javax.ws.rs.core.Request` is a helper class that can be used with conditional GETs. A client application can perform a conditional GET by sending the Last-Modified header and the `ETag` header to the server and requesting the server to send data only if the resource has been modified. The `javax.ws.rs.core.Request` has methods that compare the passed in date and/or `ETag` value and compare it with the date or `ETag` in the request header. If the headers are not present in the request or if the information in the request headers does not match the data passed in, then the methods in the Request interface return a null, otherwise they return a 200 OK Response. The `javax.ws.rs.core.Request` can be passed to a JAX-RS service method as a parameter by specifying the `@Context` annotation.

Chapter **13**

Spring REST Basics

101: Name some of the important annotations that are required while implementing a REST application via Spring.

Answer:

Spring's MVC module provides support for developing a REST application. This module provides several annotations that are useful for developing a REST application. Some of the important annotations are as follows:

a) @Controller and @RestController – A class that handles REST requests from client applications, needs to have either one of these annotations specified.

b) @RequestMapping, @GetMapping, @PostMapping, etc. – The controller class or the methods in a controller class can have these annotations specified. These annotations indicate the URI that the method maps to.

c)   `@Pathvariable, @RequestBody, @RequestParam` –
These annotations can be used on the arguments to the
methods in a REST service and specify the input parameters
to a REST service.

102: What are the steps involved in creating a REST application via Spring?

Answer:

In order to create a REST application via Spring, you need to
follow the following steps:

a)   Include JAR files for spring-mvc. If you are using Maven,
you need to add dependencies for spring-core, spring-
context, spring-webmvc and springweb.

b)   Create a REST Controller class. (This class should have the
`@RestController` or `@Controller` annotation).

c)   Add methods in the controller that service the client
requests. On each method, you need to specify the
`@RequestMapping` annotation with the URI that the
method maps to.

103: Elaborate the `@Controller` annotation.

Answer:

The `@Controller` annotation is used to designate a class as a
Spring controller that can handle incoming requests from client
applications. It needs to be specified at the class level. The
`@Controller` annotation can be used to specify a normal MVC
controller that handles web requests as well as a REST controller
that handles requests by REST clients. In order to use the
`@Controller` annotation for a REST application, you also need

to specify the @ResponeBody annotation at the class or method level.

104: Explain the differences between @Controller and @RestController.

Answer:

Both the @Controller and @RestController annotations can be used to process REST requests by REST clients. However, there are some differences between the two:

a) @Controller annotation can be used to handle normally MVC requests in which case it simple serves an HTML page as well as REST requests in which case it serves XML or JSON. The @RestController annotation on the other hand can be used only to handle REST requests.

b) When the @Controller annotation is used to handle a REST request, you also need to specify the @ResponseBody annotation. The @RestController annotation can be used by itself as it combines the @Controller and @ResponseBody annotations.

c) @RestController was added by Spring 4.0, the @Controller annotation is present in earlier versions of Spring too.

105: How can you specify the URI that a method in a Controller maps to?

Answer:

Spring provides the @RequestMapping annotation. It can be specified on a Controller class or on an individual method within the Controller. It has an attribute called path which specifies the

URI that the method maps to. If the annotation is specified at the class level, all methods in the class map to the same URL specified with this annotation. If the annotation is specified at the method level, the method level annotation overrides the class level annotation. In addition to the URI that the method maps to, the @RequestMapping annotation has another attribute called method which specifies the HTTP method that the particular method maps to. Spring also provides annotations like @GetMapping, @PostMapping etc. which can also be used on a method to specify the URI that the method maps to. These annotations correspond to the HTTP GET and POST methods respectively, so you do not need to specify the HTTP method in these annotations.

106: What is the use of the RequestParam **annotation? Write a code sample which demonstrates it.**

Answer:

The @RequestParam annotation can be used to specify parameters that are sent as query parameters in a client request. Query parameters are parameters specified using a "?" symbol after the main URL and are of the format parametername=parametervalue.

Consider the following code:

```
@GetMapping("/person")
   public Person getPersonWithId(@RequestParam
Integer personId){
       return null; // TODO - write actual code
   }
```

Here, the @RequestParam annotation is specified on the personId parameter, which indicates that a client application will send the personId as a query parameter as follows:

```
http://localhost/myapp/person?personId=1
```

107: What is the use of the `@RequestBody` **and** `@ResponseBody` **annotations?**

Answer:

The `@RequestBody` annotation can be used to automatically convert data in an HTTP request to the appropriate object. Normally when a client request sends an object data type, it sends it in either JSON or XML format. This annotation uses the data in JSON or XML format and automatically converts it to the appropriate Java object. It can be specified on an argument to a REST method. The `@ResponseBody` annotation can be used to automatically convert a Java object to the appropriate media type. This is normally specified on a method or controller class. So, it automatically converts an object returned by a REST method to JSON or XML format. If the `@RestController` annotation is used, then the `@ResponseBody` annotation need not be used, the data will automatically be converted to the appropriate media type.

108: What is an `HttpMessageConverter` **used for in Spring REST?**

Answer:

An `HttpMessageConverter` is an interface that helps to convert data to the appropriate mime type like JSON, XML, etc. There are several implementations of this interface like `Jaxb2CollectionHttpMessageConverter`, `MappingJackson2HttpMessageConverter`, etc. Each implementation has one or more mime types associated with it and can be used to convert the data into the correct mime type.

For example, the
`Jaxb2CollectionHttpMessageConverter` can be used to
convert data to an XML data type. When the client application
sends a request, Spring checks the "`Accept`" header in the
request to determine the data type that the client is able to
understand and accordingly uses the appropriate converter to
convert the data to the correct type that the client can understand.

**109: How does Spring REST support the HATEOAS REST
principle?**

Answer:

HATEOAS stands for Hypermedia As The Engine Of Application
State. This principle allows embedding links to other resources or
services in a REST response, so the client application need not
initially know about the services provided by a REST application,
as and when it requests a service, links to other related services
are sent in the response to the client application. Spring provides
the HATEOAS support in a separate Jar file, so in order to be able
to use HATEOAS in your application, you first need to add the Jar
file. If you are using Maven, you need to add the dependency
`org.springframework.hateoas`. Secondly, Spring provides
a class called `ResourceSupport`, your resource representation
class needs to extend this class. So for example, if you have a class
called Person that stores person details, the `Person` class needs to
extend the `ResourceSupport` class.

Chapter **14**

Spring REST Request Processing

110: Explain the attributes of the `@RequestMapping`
annotation.

Answer:

The `@RequestMapping` annotation can specified on a Controller
class or on any method within a controller. It has the following
attributes:

a) `path` – specifies the URI path that the class/method maps to

b) `method` – specifies the HTTP method that the class/method
    can handle

c) `headers` – This specifies the headers in the request which
    the class/method can accept

d) `consumes` – This specifies the type of data that the

class/method can accept

e) produces – This specifies the type of data that the class/method can produce

f) params – Specifies the parameters that can be present in the incoming request

g) value – This is an alias for the path attribute

111: What will happen if the method attribute is not specified with the @RequestMapping **annotation?**

Answer:

The method attribute on the @RequestMapping annotation specifies the HTTP method that the class or method maps to. If it is not specified, then the class or method can map to all of the HTTP methods, that is GET, POST, PUT, HEAD, DELETE etc. So, the method attribute is added only to narrow down the HTTP method that the method or class can handle. For example, consider the following code:

```
@RequestMapping("/hello")
 public String helloWorld() {
    System.out.println("In
HelloWorldController");
   String message = "Hello World";
   return message;
 }
```

Here, the method attribute is not specified, so the helloWorld method can map to any HTTP method that specifies /hello in the URI.

112: Explain the `@GetMapping` **annotations.**

Answer:

The `@GetMapping` is a shortcut annotations added by Spring 4.3. Prior to Spring 4.3, if you wanted to map a method to an HTTP GET method, you would need to write code similar to the following:

```
@RequestMapping(value="/person/{personId}",
method=RequestMethod.GET)
  public Person getPersonWithId(@PathVariable
Integer personId){
  // code here
  }
```

Here, the `@RequestMapping` annotation is used on the `getPersonWithId` method. It maps to the `/person/{personId}` URL. The method attribute is also specified. This indicates that this method maps to an HTTP GET request.

This same code can be re-written using the `@GetMapping` annotation as follows:

```
@GetMapping("/person/{personId}")
public Person getPersonWithId(@PathVariable
Integer personId){
}
```

This code uses the `@GetMapping` annotation instead of the `@RequestMapping` annotation. The method attribute is not specified since the `@GetMapping` always maps to an HTTP Get method.

113: Explain the differences between `@RequestMapping` **and** `@PostMapping`.

Answer:

Both the `@RequestMapping` and `@PostMapping` annotations can be used to map a URI to a method or a controller class and to specify the HTTP method to be used for mapping. However, there are some differences between the two:

a) The `@RequestMapping` can be used with any HTTP method. It has a method attribute that can be used to specify the HTTP method that the particular class or method maps to. If the method attribute is skipped, it means that the class or method that has this annotation can handle all the HTTP methods. The `@PostMapping` annotation on the other hand caters to only an HTTP POST method, so you do not need to specify the HTTP method.

b) The `@PostMapping` annotation was added in Spring 4.3, the `@RequestMapping` annotation is present right from the start.

114: Write a sample code that handles a Get request via Spring REST.

Answer:

The following is a code sample that demonstrates a GET request via Spring REST:

```
@RestController
public class HelloWorldController {
  @GetMapping("/hello")
  public String helloWorld() {
      System.out.println("In
HelloWorldController");
```

```
    String message = "Hello World";
    return message;
  }
}
```

Here, there is a class called `HelloWorldController`. It has the `@RestController` annotation specified indicating that it is a REST controller. There is a single method called `helloWorld`. It has the `@GetMapping` annotation which indicates that this method corresponds to an HTTP Get method. The URI "/hello" is specified in the `GetMapping` annotation which indicates that this method maps to this URI. So, when a client application invokes the /hello URL, the text "Hello World" will be returned to the client.

115: Explain the differences between `@Get` annotation and `@GetMapping` annotation.

Answer:

Both the Get and `@GetMapping` annotation can be used to cater to an HTTP GET request. However, there are several differences between the two:

a) `@Get` annotation is part of JAX-RS specification, `@GetMapping` is a Spring annotation.

b) In order to specify the type of data that the method produces or type of data that the method accepts, you need to use the `@Produces` annotation or the `@Consumes` annotation with the `@Get` annotation. However, the `@GetMapping` annotation has attribute called "produces" and "consumes" which can be used to specify the type of data that the method can produce or accept.

116: What is the use of the `@PathVariable` annotation?

Answer:

The `@PathVariable` annotation is used to specify request parameters that are specified as part of the URI. The following code demonstrates this:

```
@GetMapping("/person/{personId}")
  public Person getPersonWithId(@PathVariable
Integer personId){
      return null; // TODO - write actual code
  }
```

Here, the `getPersonWithId` method has the `@GetMapping` annotation specified. The `personId` parameter is specified in the URI itself. The `@PathVariable` annotation is used with the `personId` parameter to indicate that this parameter will be sent as part of the URI. A client application needs to send the `personId` parameter as follows:

`http://localhost/myapp/getperson/1`

Here, the value 1 is specified as the path variable and will be assigned to the `personId` parameter.

117: Explain the differences between `@PathVariable` and `@RequestParam` annotations.

Answer:

Both the `@RequestParam` and `@PathVariable` annotations can be used to extract data from the client request. However, there are some differences between the two:

a) The `@PathVariable` annotation is used to extract request parameters sent as part of the URI. Example:

`http://localhost/myapp/getperson/1` -

Here 1 specifies the id of the `person` object whose details are required. The @RequestParam annotation on the other hand is used to extract request parameters that are sent as query parameters. Example: http://localhost/myapp/getperson?id=1. Here, the id 1 is sent as a query parameter.

b) The @PathVariable annotation is more suited for REST applications, the @RequestParam annotation is more suitable for a traditional web application.

118: How can you specify multiple URI paths with a @RequestMapping **annotation?**

Answer:

The @RequestMapping annotation can be used to map a method in a Controller class to an appropriate HTTP method. It also specifies the URI that the method maps to. It has an attribute known as value This can be used to specify the URI to which the method maps. If multiple values need to be specified, they can be specified as a comma separated list. The following code demonstrates this:

```
@RequestMapping(value={"/path1","/path2"})
public String myMethod(){
  return "myMethod";
}
```

Here, the myMethod has the @RequestMapping annotation specified. It is mapped to 2 URIs, /path1 and /path2. So, any client request that has either of these values will be mapped to this method.

119: What is the use of the headers attribute in the
`@GetMapping` **annotation? Explain with an example.**

Answer:

The headers attribute in the `@GetMapping` annotation can be
used to specify the headers that need to be present in the incoming
request in order for the method to be invoked. In other words, it is
used to narrow down the requests which can invoke the method
that has the `@GetMapping` annotation. The following code
demonstrates this:

```
@GetMapping(value="/person",
headers="hname=hval")
  public Person getPerson(){
   return null;
  }
```

Here, the `getPerson` has the `@GetMapping` annotation
specified with the header attribute. Here a header with name
`hname` and value `hvalue` is specified. So only incoming requests
that include this header will be mapped to the `getPerson`
method.

120: How can you specify a default value for a request
parameter? Explain with a code sample.

Answer:

The `@RequestMapping` annotation has an attribute called
`defaultValue`. You can use this attribute to specify a default
value for a request parameter. So, when the client application does
not send a value for the request parameter, the default value
specified here will be used. The following code demonstrates this:

```
@GetMapping("/person/")
public Person
getPersonWithId(@RequestParam(defaultValue=2)
```

```
Integer personId) {
        // Code here
}
```

Here, the @RequestParam annotation is specified on the personId parameter. The defaultValue attribute is specified with the @RequestParam annotation with the value 2. So when the client application does not send a value for the personId, the value 2 will be passed to this method.

This page is intentionally left blank

Chapter **15**

Spring REST Response Processing

121: What is the use of the `ResponseEntity` **class?**

Answer:

The `ResponseEntity` class can be used to customise the response sent to a client application. It is a sub-class of `HttpEntity` class. The `HttpEntity` class represents the Http headers and body of either an HTTP request or response. The `ResponseEntity` extends `HttpEntity` by including a status code. So, you can control the HTTP status code, the Response headers and response body via the `ResponseEntity` annotation. So instead of returning an actual object, the Spring REST method can return a `ResponseEntity` instance with the appropriate data set in it. The `ResponseEntity` is a generic class, so can be used for any datatype. So, for example, if your method returns a String value and you want it to customize the response sent, you can return `ResponseEntity<String>` from the method.

122: Write a code sample that demonstrates the `@RequestBody` **annotation.**

Answer:

The `@RequestBody` annotation is used to automatically convert data sent by a client application in XML or JSON format to a Java object. The following code demonstrates this:

```
@PostMapping("/person/newperson")
 public void addPerson(@RequestBody Person
person){
     //code here


   }
```

Here, the `@RequestBody` annotation is used with the `Person` object passed in to the `addPerson` method. So, a client application can send `Person` data in XML or JSON format as follows:

XML Format

```
<person>
<name>Bill</name>
<age>20</age>
 </person>
```

JSON format

```
{ "name":"Bill",  "age":"20" }
```

The `@RequestBody` annotation is responsible for converting this data to a `Person` object.

123: When can the `@ResponseBody` annotation be skipped?

Answer:

The `@ResponseBody` annotation can be used to automatically convert a Java object to the appropriate format like JSON or XML and written directly to the response stream. It can be specified at the class level or method level. This annotation can be skipped if the `@RestController` annotation is specified on the class instead of the Controller annotation. The `@RestController` annotation was added by Spring 4.0 and it combines the behaviour of the `@Controller` and `@ResponseBody` annotations. So basically, when the `@RestController` annotation is used, the data returned by the methods in the controller is automatically converted to the appropriate format and written to the response stream, so there is no need for the `@ResponseBody` annotation.

124: What is the `ResponseEntity.BodyBuilder` interface?

Answer:

The `ResponseEntity` class can be used to customise the response sent to a client application. So, you can control the HTTP status code, the Response headers and response body. The `ResponseEntity.BodyBuilder` is a nested interface within the `ResponseEntity` class. It is used to create the response body. It has a method called body; this returns a `ResponseEntity` with the body set in it. It also has methods called `contentLength` which sets the length of the body in bytes and `contentType` which sets the content type of the response.

125: What is the use of the `ResponseEntity.ok` **method? Write a code sample that demonstrates this method.**

Answer:

The `ResponseEntity.ok` is a static method on the `ResponseEntity` class. This method is generally used to create a `ResponseEntity` with the HTTP status 200 which means that the request has been processed successfully. It returns a `ResponseEntity.BodyBuilder` instance corresponding to status code 200. The following code sample demonstrates this:

```
@RequestMapping("/hello")
public ResponseEntity<String> helloWorld() {
  String message = "Hello World";
  ResponseEntity<String> responseEntity =
  ResponseEntity.ok(message);
  return responseEntity;
}
```

Here, the `helloWorld` method returns a `ResponseEntity<String>` instance. The `ResponseEntity.ok` method is used which creates a `ResponseEntity` with the specified String value.

126: How can you create a `ResponseEntity` **with a particular status code?**

Answer:

There are several methods on the `ResponseEntity` class that let you create a `ResponseEntity` object with a particular status code:

a) `ResponseEntity.status(int status)` – This accepts an integer status code and returns a `ResponseEntity.BodyBuilder` instance with the specified status.

b) `ResponseEntity.status(HttpStatus status)` – This accepts an enum value of the `HttpStatus` type and returns a `ResponseEntity.BodyBuilder` instance with the specified status.

In addition, there are several methods on the `ResponseEntity` class that create `ResponseEntity.BodyBuilder` instances with particular status codes. For example, the `ResponseEntity.ok` creates a `ResponseEntity.BodyBuilder` with the code as 200, the `Response.accepted` creates a `ResponseEntity.BodyBuilder` with the code as 202.

127: Write a code sample that demonstrates how you can set a header in a `ResponseEntity` class.

Answer:

The following code demonstrates creating and setting a custom header in the `ResponseEntity` class:

```
@RequestMapping("/setheaderdemo")
public ResponseEntity<String> setHeader() {
  String message = "Hello World";
  HttpHeaders responseHeaders = new
  HttpHeaders();
  responseHeaders.set("CustomHeader",
  "CustomValue");
  ResponseEntity<String> responseEntity = new
  ResponseEntity<String>(message,
  responseHeaders, HttpStatus.OK);
  return responseEntity;
}
```

There is a class called `HttpHeaders` supported by Spring. This can be used to represent a request or response headers. It has a method called set, which can be used to create a header. The `set` method accepts `Strings` corresponding to the header name and header value. Here, a new object called `responseHeaders` of type `HttpHeaders` is created and the `responseHeaders.set` method is invoked with a custom header name and header value. A new `ResponseEntity` is then created with the response body (which is a String value here), the response headers just created and the HTTP status code corresponding to OK status.

128: Write a code sample that demonstrates a Spring REST method that produces a text response.

Answer:

The following code demonstrates a REST method that produces a plain text output:

```
@RequestMapping(value="/hello", produces = {
"text/plain" })
public String helloWorld() {
  System.out.println("In
  HelloWorldController");
  String message = "Hello World";
  return message;
}
```

Here, the `helloWorld` method has the `@RequestMapping` annotation specified. In addition to the value attribute which specifies the URI that this method maps to, the produces attribute is also specified on the `RequestMapping` annotation with the value "`text/plain`". This indicates that this method produces a text output. Within the method itself, a String value is returned.

129: What is the use of the `@ResponseStatus` **annotation?**

Answer:

The `@ResponseStatus` annotation can be used to specify the response status code to be sent to a client. By default, Spring sends an appropriate HTTP status code. So, if a method completes successfully, it sends the HTTP 200 status code, however if there is an error, it sends the appropriate status code. However, if you want to explicitly specify the status code that a method should return, you need to specify this annotation. So, it has an attribute called `code`, where you need to specify the actual status code. It also has an attribute called "`reason`", where you can specify a text String which is the reason for sending that status code. This annotation can be specified on a controller method or an exception handler. If it is specified on an exception handler, the exception handler method will send the response code specified when the particular exception occurs.

130: What is the use of the `consumes` **attribute on the** `@RequestMapping` **annotation? Explain with a code sample.**

Answer:

The consumes attribute on the `@RequestMapping` annotation specifies the content type of data that the method can accept. Consider the following code snippet:

```
@RequestMapping(value = "/person/newperson1",
consumes="application/xml")
  public void addPerson(@RequestBody Person
  person) {
  }
```

Here, the consumes attribute is specified on the `@RequestMapping` annotation on the `addPerson` method.

This indicates that this method can only accept client requests that send the data in XML format. So, if client application sends the data in some other format like JSON, the client request will not be mapped to this method.

Chapter **16**

Spring REST Exception Handling

131: What are the different ways in which you can achieve exception handling in a Spring REST application?

Answer:

There are several ways in which exception handling can be done in a Spring REST application. The first approach is the `ExceptionHandler` approach. In this approach, you can designate a method in your controller with the `@ExceptionHandler` annotation. You can specify some exceptions with this annotation, so when those exceptions occur, the code in the method will be executed. The downside to this approach is that, the exception handling method can only handle exceptions that occur in the controller in which the exception hander is defined. The other way is to have a class with the

@ControllerAdvice annotation with exception handling methods. This acts like a global exception handler, so exceptions thrown by any part of the code can be handled by this class. The third approach is using the ResponseStatusException. Whenever an exception occurs in your code, you can create a ResponseStatusException with the appropriate HTTP error code and throw this exception.

132: Explain with a code sample how exception handling can be done via the @ExceptionHandler annotation.

Answer:

The @ExceptionHandler annotation can be applied to a method in a controller class. It marks the method on which it is applied as an exception handling method. Along with the annotation you need to specify the exceptions that the method handles. So, when an exception occurs, the method marked as ExceptionHandler with the particular exception specified will be executed.

The following code demonstrates this:

```
ExceptionHandler(NullPointerException.class)
  public void onNullPointerException(){
    System.out.println("In
    onNullPointerException exception handler ");
  }
```

Here, the onNullPointerException method is designated as an exception handler method. So, whenever a NullPointerException is thrown by a method in the code, this method will get executed.

**133: Write a code sample that demonstrates how the
@ResponseStatus annotation can be used to send an error
corresponding to HTTP status code 500.**

Answer:

The @ResponseStatus annotation can be specified on a method
designated with the @ExceptionHandler annotation. Within
this annotation, you can specify the status code that you want to
send to the client application whenever the particular exception
occurs. The following code demonstrates how this annotation can
be used to send an error code corresponding to HTTP status 500:

```
@ExceptionHandler(NullPointerException.class)
@ResponseStatus(HttpStatus.INTERNAL_SERVER_ERROR)
  public void
onNullPointerException(NullPointerException npe){
    // code here
  }
```

Here, the @ResponseStatus annotation is specified on the
onNullPointerException method. So, whenever a
NullPointerException occurs, this method will be executed
and status code for Internal Server Error which is 500 will be sent
to the client application.

**134: What are the limitations on using the
@ExceptionHandler annotation for handling exceptions in a
Spring REST application? How can you overcome these
limitations?**

Answer:

The @ExceptionHandler annotation can be applied to a
method in a controller class and handles only exceptions that
occur in the controller class where it is specified. The downside to
this is that you will need separate exception handler methods in

every controller and this may result in code duplication. In order to avoid this, Spring provides an alternate approach where you can designate a class with the `@ControllerAdvice` annotation. Within this class, you can have methods that handle individual exceptions with the `@ExceptionHandler` annotation. So, exceptions thrown from anywhere in your application will be handled by the methods in this class.

135: What are the types or arguments that can be passed to a method that has the `@ExceptionHandler` annotation and what should be the return type of such a method?

Answer:

An Exception handling method can have any type of arguments. So, it can accept one or more exception objects of the type of exceptions that it can handle. It can also have the request or response object as an argument. The return type of an exception handling method can also be of any data type. It can also be a `Model` or `ModelAndView` object. If the method returns void, it means that the exception handling method directly writes to the response stream.

136: What are the advantages of `ResponseStatusException`?

Answer:

The `ResponseStatusException` class represents an exception. It can be used to communicate to a client application that an exception has occurred. It allows creating an Exception instance by supplying the HTTP status code that corresponds to the exception. The advantage of using this class is that the exception class is not tied down to any particular status code, so you can use different status codes for the same exception, depending on the context in which the exception occurs. This is much better than the `ExceptionHandler` approach where the exception handling method can only handle the listed exceptions and also use only a single status code which is specified in the `ResponseStatus` annotation. Secondly, you do not need to create any custom exception classes, you can use this class as required with appropriate status codes.

137: Write a code sample that demonstrates how you can do exception handling via the `ResponseStatusException`.

Answer:

The `ResponseStatusException` class represents an exception. It can be used to communicate to a client application that an exception has occurred. The following code sample demonstrates this:

```
@GetMapping(value = "/person")
  public Person getPerson() {
    try {
      throw new NullPointerException();
    } catch (NullPointerException npe)
{
      throw new
      ResponseStatusException(HttpStatus.INTERNA
      L_SERVER_ERROR, "NullPointerException
      occured");
    }
  }
```

Here, the `getPerson` method explicitly throws a `NullPointerException`. There is a `try/catch` block that catches this exception and creates and throws a `ResponseStatusException`. The `ResponseStatusException` is created with the Http status code for Internal Server Error and a String message that states that an error has occurred.

138: How can @ControllerAdvice be used to handle exceptions? Explain with a code sample.

Answer:

The @ControllerAdvice annotation can be applied to a class. Within the class, you can have different exception handling methods annotated with the @ExceptionHandler annotation. So, when an exception occurs in any part of the code, it will be handled by the corresponding method in the class with @ControllerAdvice annotation. The following code demonstrates this:

```
@ControllerAdvice
public class MyExceptonHandler {
  @ExceptionHandler(NullPointerException.class)
@ResponseStatus(HttpStatus.INTERNAL_SERVER_ERROR)
  public void
  onNullPointerException(NullPointerException npe){
    System.out.println("In onNullPointerException
    exception handler ");
  }
@ExceptionHandler(IllegalArgumentException.class)
  @ResponseStatus(HttpStatus.BAD_REQUEST)
  public void
  onIllegaArgumentException(IllegalArgumentException
  npe){
    System.out.println("In onNullPointerException
    exception handler ");
  }
}
```

Here, the MyExceptionHandler class has the @ControllerAdvice annotation specified. It has 2 methods, onNullPointerException and

onIllegaArgumentException. So, if a
NullPointerException occurs anywhere in your code, the
onNullPointerException method will be invoked and the
Http status code corresponding to internal server error will be
sent to the client application. Similarly, if an
IllegalArgumentException occurs anywhere in your code,
the onIllegaArgumentException method will be invoked
and the Http status code corresponding to Bad Request will be
sent to the client application.

**139: What is the use of the
ResponseEntityExceptionHandler?**

Answer:

Spring has some standard exceptions which it throws when some
common errors occur like invalid request parameter, malformed
request sent by client application, etc. All these exceptions are
handled by this ResponseEntityExceptionHandler class.
So, this class has several methods that have the
@ExceptionHandler annotation specified. Each method
accepts a parameter that is an exception object of the type of
exceptions that the method handles. All the methods return a
ResponseEntity instance. If you want to customize the error
message sent to a client application when any of these standard
exceptions occur, you can create a sub-class of this class and
override the corresponding method.

140: What is the MediaTypeNotSupportedException?
Answer:

The MediaTypeNotSupportedException is a sub-class of
the ResponseStatusException. It corresponds to the HTTP

status code 415. It can be thrown by application code when the media type specified in the accept header in the incoming request is not supported by the REST service. So, for example if the accept header specifies "text/html", but there is no method that matches the URI and produces html output, then this exception can be thrown by the application code. It has two constructors; one constructor accepts a List of supported media types and creates a `MediaTypeNotSupportedException` with this list. The second constructor creates a `MediaTypeNotSupportedException` with a String value which is the reason for the exception.

Chapter **17**

Spring REST Client

141: What are the different ways in which you can create a client application for a Spring REST service?

Answer:

There are several ways in which you can create a client application that consumes a Spring REST service. Also, it is not mandatory to use Spring on the client side, you can use any other framework too. For example, you can use `HttpConnection` class which is an in-built class in JDK. You can use a JAX-RS implementation like Jersey or RESTEasy in order to create a REST client application. You can use Apache HTTP client. If at all you want to use Spring, Spring also provides support for creating a REST client via its spring-web module. This module has a class called `RestTemplate` which can be used to create a client application.

142: What is the use of the `RestTemplate` class?

Answer:

`RestTemplate` is a class in Spring Web and is the starting point in creating a REST client application. It uses the URI and the HTTP method to invoke in order to connect to a REST service. It has various methods that can be used for various HTTP calls. Some of the methods on this class are `getForEntity` which is used to perform an HTTP GET on the specified URI, the `postForEntity` which can be used to perform an HTTP POST, the put method that can be used to perform a PUT operation, the exchange method which can be used to execute any HTTP method, etc.

143: Write a code sample that demonstrates the `RestTemplate.getForEntity` method.

Answer:

`RestTemplate` class can be used by a Spring client application to query a REST service. The `getForEntity` method can be used to retrieve information via a GET request. The following code demonstrates this:

```
RestTemplate restTemplate = new
RestTemplate();
ResponseEntity<String> response =
restTemplate.getForEntity(URI, String.class);
System.out.println("Response is
"+response.getBody());
```

The `restTemplate.getForEntity` method accepts the server URI and a class instance of the data type that the server method returns. In this case, a `String.class` is used. It returns a `ResponseEnity` of the data type that the server application returns. The `responseEntity.getBody` method can be used to retrieve the actual response body from the `ResponseEntity`

144: How can a Spring REST client application retrieve header information? Explain with a code sample.

Answer:

There are several methods on the `RestTemplate` class that can be used by a client application to retrieve header information. One such method is the `headForHeaders`. This method performs an HTTP HEAD request. The following code demonstrates this:

```
HttpHeaders headers =
restTemplate.headForHeaders(ROOT_URI);
```

The `headForHeaders` method accepts the URI of the REST service. It returns an instance of `HttpHeaders` which stores key-value pairs corresponding to the actual headers. So, there are methods on the `HttpHeaders` class using which you can retrieve a header value using its name. There are several overloaded versions of the `headForHeaders` method. So along with the server URI, you can pass in a Map of parameter names and values for the URI, etc.

145: How can you specify parameter values while performing an HTTP GET in a Spring REST client application?

Answer:

The `RestTemplate` class has a `getForEntity` method that can be used to retrieve information via a GET request. This method accepts the server URI and a class instance corresponding to the response type. In addition, it has some overloaded versions that accepts the parameters as follows:

```
getForEntity(String url, Class<T> responseType, Map
<String,?> uriVariables)
```

In addition to the URI and class instance of the response, this method accepts a map which specifies the query parameter names and values.

```
getForEntity(String url, Class<T> responseType,
Object... uriVariables)
```

In addition to the URI and class instance of the response, this method accepts a variable number of values corresponding to the parameters.

So, these methods can be used to pass in the parameter values while performing a GET operation.

146: What is the difference between the `postForEntity,` `postForObject` **and** `postForLocation` **methods?**

Answer:

All three methods, that is `postForEntity`, `postForObject` and `postForLocation` are methods on the `RestTemplate` class and can be used to perform an HTTP POST request. The `postForEntity` and `postForObject` methods should be used when you want to save some data on the server whereas the `postForLocation` should be used when you want to create a new resource on the server. The `postForEntity` method returns a `ResponseEntity`, the `postForObject` method returns an actual object and the `postForLocation` method returns a URI of the newly created resource. The `ResponseEntity` returned by `postForEntity` includes the response headers and response status in addition to actual object, so this method should be used when you want the Response headers or response status. When you only need the object returned by the method, you can use the `postForObject` method. Both `postForEntity` and `postForObject` method accept as parameter a class instance of the data type that the method returns. The `postForLocation` does not accept a class instance as it returns a URI.

147: What is the use of the `RequestEntity` class?

Answer:

The `RequestEntity` class is a sub-class of the `HttpEntity` class. The `HttpEntity` class represents an HTTP Request or Response and includes the request/response headers and body. The `RequestEntity` goes a step further and stores the HTTP method to be used and the URI to be invoked as well. There are several static methods on this class like get, post, etc. which can be used to create a `RequestEntity` with the corresponding HTTP method. The `RequestEntity` class is generally used in the `RestTemplate.exchange` method where it is passed as a parameter.

148: Write a sample code that demonstrates how you can perform a delete operation via a Spring REST client.

Answer:

The `RestTemplate` class which can be used by a Spring client application to query a REST service has a delete method that can be used to execute an HTTP delete request. The following code demonstrates this:

```
restTemplate.delete(ROOT_URI);
```

The `delete` method accepts the URI of the resource that needs to be deleted. In addition to this `delete` method, there are several overloaded versions of the `delete` method that can be used to pass path variables in the URI. None of the `delete` methods return any value, they return a void.

149: What is the use of the `resttemplate.exchange` **method?**

Answer:

The `RestTemplate.exchange` method can also be used by a client application to invoke an HTTP method on the server. It accepts a `RequestEntity` instance as a parameter and returns a `ResponseEntity`. The `RequestEntity` carries information about the URI to be invoked, the HTTP method to be used and the data to be sent as part of the request. So, it invokes the REST service as per the data in the `RequestEntity` and wraps the data returned by the service as a `ResponseEntity`. In addition to `RequestEntity`, the exchange method may accept other parameters like a class instance corresponding to the return data type, explicit URI to be invoked, HTTP method to be used, etc. There are several overloaded versions of this method that slightly differ in the input parameters

150: Explain the `WebClient` **interface.**

Answer:

`WebClient` is an interface added by Spring 5. It is an alternate to `RestTemplate` and can be used by a client application to invoke a REST service. It is part of the Spring Web Reactive module and in order to use it, you need to add `spring-webflux` to your Maven file. `WebClient` is a non-blocking client and so can be used for asynchronous calls as well. So, a client application that uses `WebClient` does not have to wait for the response, it gets notified when the Response is available. `WebClient` has several methods like `get`, `post`, etc. which can be used to perform the corresponding HTTP operations.

Chapter **18**

JSON

151: What is JSON? Why was it developed?

Answer:

JSON stands for JavaScript Object Notation. It uses JavaScript syntax. It is a data storage and communication protocol. JSON is used primarily in REST services to transfer data. It stores data in the form of key-value pairs. Before JSON was developed, XML was used to exchange data between a REST client and a REST server. However, the downside to this is that XML is very verbose. JSON was initially created for communication between browsers and server side technology. However, it quickly emerged as an alternative to XML and started being used in REST technologies. Data sent via JSON is concise and easy to read. The media type in HTTP communication for JSON is Application/JSON.

152: Explain the main features of JSON due to which developers prefer to use it.

Answer:

JSON is a lightweight, language independent transfer protocol that can be used to interchange data between a REST service and a REST client. It is an alternative to XML. Compared to XML, it is less verbose. It is independent of the underlying platform or programming language. It is text based and therefore easy for humans to read and write. It is easy to encode and decode. It is supported by almost all platforms and programming languages like Java, PHP, JavaScript etc. Due to all this, developers prefer to use JSON.

153: What are the similarities between JSON and XML?

Answer:

There are many similarities between JSON and XML as follows:

a) Both JSON and XML can be used to represent some data.

b) Both are used as the data exchange formats between a REST server and REST client.

c) Both are language/technology independent, so irrespective of the programming language or technology used, these can be used.

d) Both are easy to read and understand for humans.

e) Both are hierarchical and support values within values.

f) Both support Unicode and thus internationalization.

g) Both are supported by all the major Java REST technologies like JAX-RS, Spring REST, etc.

154: What are the differences between JSON and XML?

Answer:

Both JSON and XML can be used to represent some data and are used as the data exchange formats in a REST application. However, there are several differences between the two:

a) JSON is easy to read and write, XML on the other hand is verbose.

b) Unlike XML, JSON does not have start and end tags.

c) You can easily specify arrays in JSON, XML does not support arrays.

d) JSON is easier to parse than XML.

e) XML is more secure than JSON.

f) Parsing XML is quick, parsing XML is slow and consumes a lot of memory.

g) JSON only supports text and numerical data types, XML also supports data types like images, charts, etc.

155: What are the data types supported by JSON?

Answer:

JSON supports the following data types:

a) **String** – This is used to represent a sequence of characters, that is a text value like "Hello".

b) **Number** – this is used to represent a numerical value like 12 or 4.5.

c) **Boolean** – This is used to represent a true/false value.

d) **Null** – This is used to represent a null value.

e) **Object** – This is used to represent an object. An object can consist of multiple fields. For example, you can have an

Employee object with employee id, employee name, etc.

f) **Array** – This is used to represent a sequence of values. The values within the array can be of any type like Number, String or Object.

156: Explain JSON syntax.

Answer:

JSON uses name value pairs separated by a colon to represent data. The left side of the colon represents the name and the right side represents its value. The name needs to be enclosed in double quotes. In addition to simple name value pairs, JSON also supports objects and arrays. If you need to represent an object via JSON, you need to enclose the object in curly brackets. Finally, if you want to represent an array of values, you need to specify the values in square brackets.

157: Explain the JSON object syntax in detail.

Answer:

JSON object is a data type supported by JSON. It corresponds to a JAVA object. A JSON object needs to be enclosed in curly brackets. Each field in the object must be represented as a key-value pair with the key being a String value corresponding to the field name and the value being a valid JSON data type (String, number, Boolean, Null, Object or Array). If the value is an object, it must be enclosed in curly brackets and must follow the same syntax. The key and the value must be separated by a colon. The key-value pairs corresponding to fields must be separated by commas.

158: Explain the JSON array syntax in detail.

Answer:

JSON array is a data type supported by JSON and is used to represent a list of values. The values within the array can be of any JSON data type like String, Number, Boolean, Null, Object or Array. Arrays must be enclosed within square brackets. The values within the array must be separated by commas. If the array stores String values, each value must be enclosed by double quotes. If the array stores objects, each object must be enclosed within curly brackets.

159: What limitations does JSON have?

Answer:

JSON can be used to represent some data and is used as the data exchange formats in a REST application. It is easier to read and less verbose than XML. However, it has some limitations as follows:

a) JSON does not support data types like image or rich text format, it only supports text and numerical data types.

b) JSON is less secure as compared to XML.

c) In XML, you can define a schema via a DTD file and validate that the XML conforms to the DTD. However, in JSON, there is no such support for formal grammar definition so it is difficult to communicate and enforce the structure of the JSON file .

d) JSON does not support comments like XML.

160: Write a code sample that demonstrates a Java class and the corresponding JSON value for it.

Answer:

Suppose you have an `Employee` class as follows:

```
public class Employee {
private int id;
  private String firstName;
  private String lastName;
}
```

And suppose we create an `Employee` as follows:

```
Employee employee = new Employee(5, "Jane", "Doe");
```

This information can be represented via JSON as follows:

```
{"id":5, "firstName":"Jane",  "lastName":"Doe"}
```

So basically, the `employee` object is wrapped around curly brackets. Each field in the object is represented as a name value pair. String values are enclosed in quotes. Each name-value pair is separated by a comma.

161: Write a Java class that corresponds to a Book object with fields for book id, book name and a List of values corresponding to book authors. Also write the JSON String that stores this information for the book with id=1, name="Book1" and authors as "Author1", "Author2".

Answer:

The following code represents a Java class corresponding to a Book:

```
public class Book {
    private int bkId;
  private String bkName;
  private List<String> bkAuthors;
```

```
    //getters and setters
}
```

The following JSON text represents the Book given in the question:

```
{"id":2 "bkName":"Book1",  "bkAuthors":
["author1","author2"]}
```

The `book` object is wrapped around curly brackets. Each field in the object is represented as a name value pair. Since the value of the `bkAuthors` field is a List, it is represented as a JSON array in square brackets. The values within the array are separated via commas.

162: Write a code sample that demonstrates how you can represent a `List` of objects via JSON.

Answer:

Suppose you have an Employee class as follows:

```
public class Employee {
  private String firstName;
  private String lastName;
}
```

And suppose we create an `Employee` list with 3 values as follows:

```
List<Employee> employees = new
ArrayList<Employee>();
employees.add(new Employee("Jane","Doe"));
employees.add(new Employee("Bill","Young"));
employees.add(new Employee("Mary","James"));
```

This can be represented in JSON as follows:

```
{
"employees":[
```

```
{"firstName":"Jane", "lastName":"Doe"},
{"firstName":"Bill", "lastName":"Young"} ,
{"firstName":"Mary", "lastName":"James"}
]

}
```

Here, our main object is the employees list, so that is enclosed within curly brackets. Within the `employees` object, we have 3 `employee` objects. Since it is a list, square brackets are used. Also, each employee object is enclosed within curly brackets and the objects are separated by a comma. Within each `employee` object, its fields are specified as name-value pairs.

163: Write a sample code that shows how you can represent a nested object in JSON.

Answer:

Suppose you have an `Employee` class as follows:

```
public class Employee {
private int id;
  private String firstName;
  private String lastName;
private Address address;
}
```

Suppose the Address class is as follows:

```
public class Address {
  private String houseNumber;
  private String streetName;
private String city;
private String pincode;
}
```

This can be represented in JSON format as follows:

```
{
```

```
"id": 2,
"firstName": "Jane",
"lastName": "Doe",
  "address" : {
    "houseNumber": "125",
    "streetName" : "MG Road",
    "city": "Pune",
    "pincode": "411001"
  }
}
```

So, within the Employee object, an address object is as another key-value pair. Since "address" is an object, it is enclosed in curly brackets. The fields of the address object are specified within the curly brackets.

This page is intentionally left blank

Chapter **19**

Postman

164: List some tools that are commonly used for testing a REST service.

Answer:

There are several tools available for testing a REST service. Some of the commonly used tools are as follows:

a) **Postman** – Postman is a very powerful tool that can be used to test REST services. It can be used to execute all the HTTP methods like GET, POST etc and supports all formats like XML, JSON, etc.

b) **SoapUI** – SoapUI is another testing tool. It can be used to test both SOAP and REST services. It has a drag and drop UI which can be used to create tests easily.

c) **Katalon Studio** – Katalon studio is a comprehensive tool that can be used for Web, Mobile and API testing. It can be used for testing both SOAP as well as REST services.

165: What is Postman?

Answer:

Postman is one of the most popular tools available for testing REST services. It was initially developed as a Chrome browser plugin but soon became available as a standalone application for all the major platforms. It can be used to test all the HTTP methods like GET, POST, etc. You can specify the request information in formats like XML or JSON. You can also specify request headers and cookies to be sent to the REST service. You can also inspect the response headers and response body sent by the REST service. In addition, it also provides several features like grouping together a number of requests and executing them together, storing common variables in environments, etc.

166: How can you test the following REST method in Postman?

Answer:

```
@GetMapping(value = "/person/")
public Person
getPersonWithId(@QueryParam("personId")
Integer personId) {
  //TODO - Code here
}
```

The above method corresponds to an HTTP GET request. It maps to the /person/ URI and accepts the personId as a query parameter. So, it will map to a URI like `http://<URI_HERE>/person?personId=2`. In order to test this method in Postman, you will need to do the following:

a)   Create a new request

b) Select the HTTP method as GET in the dropdown list of HTTP methods

c) Enter the URI of the REST service that is `http://<URI_HERE>/person` in the URI bar

d) Click on "Params" button

e) Enter the name of the parameter (personId) in the key and the value of the parameter (2) in the value

f) Click on "Send"

g) Check the Response Status and Response body in the Response pane below.

167: Explain the term, Collection, in Postman.

Answer:

A collection is simply a group of requests that is given a name. It is similar to a folder on your computer. It helps to organise your requests. You can also run all the requests within a collection at once. Whenever you create a new request, Postman may ask you to choose a Collection where you would like to save the request or create a new collection. Postman provides several features like sharing collection with team members, duplicating a collection, renaming a collection, etc.

168: What is the use of an environment variable in Postman?

Answer:

Environment variables are basically useful to store values that can be changed. It is just a key value pair where the key is the variable name and the value is the actual value. For example, suppose you have a large number of requests and different servers like development, test, production etc. Each server will have a different URI. You can store the URI as an environment variable and use this in the requests. So, if the URI changes in the future, you just need to change the value of the environment variable and not all the requests. Not only that, it makes switching between different servers like development, testing, production, easier.

169: How can you test all the methods in a Spring REST controller at once in Postman?

Answer:

Postman provides a feature called Collection Runner which can be used to test all the methods in a collection. You can use this to test all the methods in a Spring REST controller at once. First, you need to create a new collection with requests corresponding to all the methods in the controller. There is a "Runner" button in Postman, which can be used to launch the Collection Runner. Here, you can select the collection that you wish to run. There is a Collection Runner console where you can view the results of running all the requests. So, you can see if the request was successful or if it failed. You can also inspect the results of an individual request.

170: How can you define the sequence in which requests will be run by a Collection Runner?

Answer:

By default, when you add some requests to a collection and if you execute them via Collection Runner, these will get executed sequentially. However, you can change the order of execution. You can do this via the tests tab which is seen the main request window. In the tests tab, you need to specify the name of the next request that you want to execute as follows:

```
postman.setNextRequest("Next Request Name")
```

So, after the current request is completed, Postman will execute the request with the "Next Request Name".

171: How can you test the following JAX-RS REST code request via Postman?

Answer:

```
@Path("saveperson")
 @POST
 @Consumes(MediaType.APPLICATION_XML)
 public void processPerson(Person person) {
 }
```

The above method requires an HTTP POST method. It also requires the input data to be sent in XML format. So, you need to do the following:

a) Select the HTTP method as POST in the dropdown list of HTTP methods

b) Enter the URL of the REST service in the URI bar

c) Click on "Body" tab to add request body

d) Click on "Raw" and select the Media as application/xml

e) Enter the Person data in XML format

f) Click on "Send"

g) Check the Response Status and Response body in the Response pane below

172: How can you specify authentication credentials via Postman?

Answer:

Authentication is the process where a client application provides a username and password. The service checks if the credentials are correct and only if they are, it allows the client application to access the service. In postman, authentication credentials are supplied via a header. So, you need to select the "Headers" tab in the request window. In the key, you need to specify "Authorization" and in the value you need to specify the credentials, that is the username and password. The username and password must be separated by a colon. The word "basic" should be prefixed to the username and password value. So, for example if the credentials are test/test, you need to create a header as follows:

```
Authorization: "Basic test:test"
```

The credentials should be Base64 encoded. Alternatively, you can select the authorization tab, and select "Basic Auth" in the drop down. You will be prompted to enter the credentials. Once entered, Postman will automatically create the Authorization header with the Base 64 encoded values.

173: What is a Mock server in Postman?

Answer:

Just as the name suggests, a Mock server is basically a fake server that is created to simulate a real server. You can create a Mock server in Postman. Within the Mock server, you can create requests and also specify the response code/response body that you want the request to return. So, basically the mock server returns hardcoded data. You can then test the client code against this mock server. The advantage is that; you do not need a live server to do the testing. A mock server helps in identifying bugs quickly and saves time. UI developers can use a mock server before the actual service is developed. So, they do not need to wait till the actual service is developed and can start developing the UI using hardcoded data from the Mock server.

174: Write a JAX-RS method that accepts a cookie and also explain how such a method will be tested in Postman.

Answer:

The following is JAX-RS method that accepts a cookie:

```
public void myMethod(@CookieParam("myCookie")
String cookie){
//TODO - code here
}
```

Postman provides cookie support, so you can add, delete or modify cookies in Postman. Cookies are associated with a domain. So, for this example, you will need to create a cookie called "myCookie" and assign it some value. In the request window, there is a button on the top right called "Cookies". This launches the Cookie Manager. You first need to select an existing domain or create a new domain with which you want the cookie to be associated. Once you select a domain, you can click on the "Add Cookie" button. This will show you a screen where you can enter the cookie information and save it. Once you save the cookie information, the cookie is created and associated with the domain, so whenever you send a request to that domain via Postman, that cookie will also be sent.

175: How can you use Postman to check if a REST method returns 200 OK status code?

Answer:

Postman provides a "Tests" tab in the request window. So, tests are associated with a request and can be used to verify the response sent by a request, that is if the response matches certain values. You can have one or more tests associated with a request. So, in order to check if a REST method returns 200 OK status, you can create a test associated with your REST. Tests can be written either using Javascript or using a Functional method. If you are using Javascript, you will need to write code similar to the following in the "Tests" tab:

```
tests["Status 200"] = responseCode.code === 200
```

Here, the *"Status 200"* is a name given to the test. responseCode.code status code in the response. This is checked against the value 200.

Chapter **20**

Swagger

176: What are the challenges in documenting a REST application?

Answer:

Documentation is an important aspect of any project. The main challenge in documenting a REST application is that there are no established standards. SOAP based web services use a WSDL file which describes the web service and the methods defined in the web service. So, a client application can use the WSDL file and obtain a detailed description of the services provided, request and response payloads. However, in case of REST applications, there is no WSDL file, so organisations have to rely on manually created documents that describe the REST services to clients. This method is tedious and error prone.

177: What are the tools available for documenting REST services?

Answer:

There are several tools available for documenting REST services. Some of them are as follows:

a)   **WADL (Web Application Development Language)** – The WADL is a way to document HTTP web services and is the WSDL equivalent in REST.

b)   **Open API and Swagger** – This is one of the most popular tools available for documenting REST services. It allows creating interactive documentation in HTML format that is easy to read and understand. It also allows generating the documentation directly from the code.

c)   **RAML** – RAML can also be used to document REST services in HTML format. RAML provides several tools can be used to create interactive documentation or output the document into a single HTML file.

178: What is Open API?

Answer:

OPEN API is a specification that can be used to describe and document your REST services. Its current version is 3.0. Open API specification files can be written in JSON or XML format. You can document the following using Open API:

a)   Available services and HTTP operations (GET, POST, PUT, etc.) supported by each service in a REST API

b)   Input and output information for each service

c)   Authentication methods

d)   Contact information, license, terms of use and other

information.

Swagger provides a number of tools that use the Open API specification and can be used to produce interactive documentation for your web services using the Open API specification file.

179: What is Swagger?

Answer:

Swagger provides a set of tools that use the Open API specification. These tools can help to design, build, document and consume REST services. Some of the tools within Swagger are as follows:

a) **Swagger Editor** – This is a browser based editor where you can write your Open API specification document. It can be accessed via `http://editor.swagger.io`. It automatically validates the document that you are creating.

b) **Swagger UI** – Once you have the Open API specification document for your REST service, the Swagger UI can be used to display this in an interactive HTML format that is easy to read and understand for humans.

c) **Swagger Codegen** – This can be used to generate server code stubs and client libraries from an Open API specification.

180: What is the use of the Swagger Editor?

Answer:

Swagger editor can be used to create the Open API specification file. The advantage of using the Swagger editor is that it automatically validates the document that you are creating. So, you can quickly fix syntax errors if any. This is as against typing the resource file in a simple text editor, where there is no syntax checking and so it is more error prone. You can create the specification file in both JSON and YAML format in the swagger editor. The swagger editor is an online editor and can be accessed via `http://editor.swagger.io/`

181: What is Swagger UI?

Answer:

Swagger has a component called Swagger UI. It can be used to automatically generate interactive documentation for your REST API from the Open API specification file. The Open API specification file is in JSON or YAML format and not very easily readable for humans. The swagger UI converts this to an HTML format which can be accessed via a browser and so it is easy to read and understand for humans. Not only that, the document created is interactive, so you can actually run the REST requests and view the JSON/XML response sent. There are various Java libraries for Swagger UI which can be used to automatically create the interactive documentation from Java code

182: What are the basic components in an Open API specification file?

Answer:

The Open API specification file has information about the REST API using which the API can be documented via Swagger tools. The following are the main components in the specification file:

a) **Metadata** – This includes information about the Open API version used, title of the API, description of the API and version of the API.

b) **Servers** – This includes information about the servers used in the application and the base URLs of the servers. More than one server can be specified here.

c) **Paths** – This includes information about individual REST services like the URI of the service, the HTTP method supported, parameter information, request body and response body.

183: What is YAML?

Answer:

YAML stands for "YAML Ain't Markup Language." It is one of the formats in which you can write the Open API specification file which can then be used to document a REST service. Since YAML is not a markup language, it does not have markup tags like <, >. It is similar to JSON but unlike JSON, it does not have curly brackets, square brackets, etc. and so it is easier to read. YAML uses colons to denote an object's properties and hyphens to denote an array.

YAML is hierarchical and uses spaces to denote levels. Each level can store a key-value pair.

184: What are the advantages of using Swagger to document a Java REST service?

Answer:

The advantage of using Swagger to document a Java REST service is that the documentation can be generated automatically from the code. You just need to add the appropriate Swagger libraries to your REST project and may need to add some annotations to your code. Swagger then automatically generates the documentation for you in the form of the Open API specification file, which can then be rendered via the Swagger UI. The advantage of this approach is that the documentation is always in sync with the code, since the documentation is generated automatically from the code.

185: How can you create Swagger documentation automatically for a Java REST service that uses JAX-RS?

Answer:

Swagger provides a library called swagger-core which can automatically generate documentation for your JAX-RS REST service. You just need to add the dependencies for it into your JAX-RS project and it does the rest. Once you add these dependencies, the Open API specification file is automatically generated for your project is both JSON and YAML format. Swagger does this by analysing the JAX-RS or JAXB annotations in your code. In addition, swagger-core also provides its own annotations which can be used to customize the documentation.

186: Name some important annotations within Swagger-core and explain them.

Answer:

Swagger-core is a library that you can add to your JAX-RS project and once added, it analyses the JAX-RS or JAXB annotations in your code to generate the specification file. In addition, Swagger also provides its own annotations which can be used to customize the documentation. The following are some important annotations in swagger-core:

a) `@OpenAPIDefinition` – This generates the metadata for

the specification file. It can be applied at the class level.

b) `@Operation` – This can be applied to a method in your JAX-RS class and is used to customize the documentation for the method.

c) `@Parameter` – Can be applied to a parameter in an operation and is used to provide additional information about the parameter.

d) `@RequestBody` – Can be applied at the method level or within the `@Operation` annotation and is used to describe the request body.

e) `@Server` – This can be applied at the class level or within the `@Operation` annotation and is used to describe the server URL, server description, etc.

187: How can you generate the metadata section of your Open API specification using Swagger-core annotations? Demonstrate with an example.

Answer:

The metadata section consists of the Open API specification file consists of the following:

a) `OpenAPI specification version` – This specifies the Open API version that is being used.

b) `title` – This is the title of the API.

c) `description` – This is some additional information about the API. This is optional and can be skipped.

d) `version` – This is a String value which specifies the version of the API.

You can use the `@OpenAPIDefinition` annotation at the class level to generate the metadata. Within this annotation you can specify the "info" annotation with values for title, description, version, etc. The following code demonstrates this:

```
@OpenAPIDefinition(
  info = @Info(
    title = "Person API",
    version = "1.0.0",
    description = "Person API can return Person
    information, help to add a person, etc."
  )
)
```

188: Explain how a method in a REST service is documented via Swagger.

Answer:

The Open API specification file has an object called "Paths". Under this object, you can specify the URI that each REST method in your application maps to. Along with URI, you can also specify other information like the HTTP method supported, parameters accepted, responses produced, etc. By default, you do not need to specify any annotation, Swagger includes all methods that have the JAX-RS @Path annotation specified within the Paths object in the Open API specification file. However, if you want to customize the documentation for a method, you can do so by using the swagger-core @Operation annotation.

189: What is the use of the @Parameter Swagger annotation? Write a code sample that demonstrates this annotation.

Answer:

The @Parameter annotation can be specified on a method parameter or within the @Operation annotation. It can be used to add some additional information about the REST service parameter that needs to be documented. It can be used along with any of the JAX-RS parameter annotations like `@PathParam`, `@QueryParam`, `@HeaderParam`, `@CookieParam`, etc. The following code sample demonstrates this:

```
public Person getPersonById(
  @Parameter(description = "The id of the
  person whose details are required", required
  = true) @PathParam("personId") Integer
  personId) {
    // actual code here }
```

Here, the `@Parameter` annotation is used with the `personId` parameter which is a path parameter. It is used to specify the description of the parameter and whether the parameter is mandatory or not.

190: How can you use Swagger when you are developing a REST application via Spring?

Answer:

In order to use Swagger for a Spring REST application, you can use the `Springfox` library. This automatically generates the documentation for your Spring REST service. You just need to add the springfox-swagger2 and `springfox-swagger-ui` dependencies to your Maven build. This will automatically create the Open API Specification file in JSON format and also generate the interactive Swagger UI docs. The documentation can be accessed via a browser. In addition, `Springfox` library also provides its own annotations which can be added to your code to customize the generated documentation. Some of the annotations provided are `@Api`, `@ApiOperation`, etc.

191: What is the use of the `@API` **and** `@APIOperation`
annotations?

Answer:

The `@API` annotation is part of the springfox-swagger library. It
can be added on the Controller class and can be used to customize
the default documentation generated for the controller. It has
fields like description which allows you to specify some
additional information about the service. The `@ApiOperation`
can be specified on the methods in a controller and again, can be
used to customize the documentation. So, it has attributes
corresponding to description, response, etc. Both these
annotations are optional, even if they are not specified, Swagger
will still generate documentation for the REST service represented
by the controller and its methods. These annotations need to be
specified only if you want to customize the documentation or
specify additional information

Chapter **21**

Miscellaneous

192: What is WADL?

Answer:

WADL stands for Web Application Description Language. WADL is a way to document HTTP based web services and so can be used for documenting REST services. It uses the XML format. It documents the web service as a set of resource elements with information about parameters, requests and responses. It is similar to WSDL, but less verbose as compared to WSDL. It can be generated directly from code using some tools. The downside to using WADL is that it is not very easy to read and understand for humans. It is used by SoapUI which is a tool for testing both SOAP and REST web services.

193: What are the differences between a RESTful and a Restless web service?

Answer:

There are several differences between a RESTful and a RESTless web service as follows:

a) A RESTful web service follows the REST architecture whereas a RESTless web service does not follow the REST architecture.

b) A RESTful web services uses HTTP protocol, a RESTless web service uses the SOAP protocol.

c) A RESTful web service supports formats like HTML, XML, JSON, etc. whereas a RESTless service only supports XML.

d) A RESTful web service uses URIs to expose the business logic, a RESTless web service uses service interfaces to expose the business logic.

194: What does the term Payload in RESTful web services mean?

Answer:

The data exchanged between a REST server and the REST client is known as the payload. The data sent by the client to the server is known as the request payload and the data sent by a server to a client application is known as the response payload. A request payload is generally sent in in HTTP POST requests where a client application sends some data to a server. HTTP get requests generally do not include a request payload. The response payload is generally sent in case of HTTP GET requests where the client application is asking for some information. The payload can be specified in JSON or XML format.

195: What are the factors that need to be considered while choosing whether to create a SOAP or a REST service?

Answer:

The following are some of the factors that need to be taken into consideration while choosing whether to create a SOAP or a REST service:

a) If the service exposes data, REST should be chosen, if it exposes business logic SOAP should be chosen.

b) If you need a formal contract between the client and server application, then you need to choose SOAP as it provides such a formal contract via WSDL.

c) If you need to support various data formats like HTML, XML, JSON, you need to choose REST since SOAP does not support multiple data formats.

d) If your application needs a high level of security, you need to choose SOAP as it provides a higher level of security than REST.

e) Overall, a REST application is easier to develop, test and maintain.

196: How can a REST API be versioned?

Answer:

There are several approaches that can be used to version a REST API. These are as follows:

a) **URL Versioning** – In this approach, the version information is stored as part of the URI. For example, the URIs `http://server.com/v1/persons` and `http://server.com/v2/persons` refer to 2 different versions of the Person API.

b) **URI Parameter versioning** – This is similar to URI versioning except that the version is specified as a query parameter in the URI. So `http://server.com/persons?version=v1` and `http://server.com/v2/persons?version=v2` use the version parameter to specify different versions of the REST API.

c) **Accept Header versioning** – In this approach, the "Accept-Header" is used to specify the version information with a custom media type.

d) **Custom header versioning** – Here a custom header can be used to specify the version. So, a client application can specify the version that it needs via this custom header.

197: Why should pagination be used in a REST service?

Answer:

A REST API can have different types of clients like web, mobile or desktop applications. Sometimes a REST API may send large amount of data. Sending large amount of data at once can cause bandwidth and performance issues. This is particularly true for mobile applications. So, in such scenarios, sending data in small chunks proves to be more efficient. A client application can process the chunk of data sent to it and then fetch the next chunk in a separate request.

198: How can you achieve pagination in a REST application?

Answer:

There are several approaches in which pagination can be achieved in a REST application. One approach is to let the client application specify the page number and the REST service can only return the results corresponding to that page number. Another approach is where a client application can specify two parameters, a limit and an offset. The limit parameter indicates the maximum results to return and offset parameter indicates the starting point from which to return the data. Or a client application can also use time based pagination where they can specify a time frame to retrieve the data.

199: In addition to the actual data, what data must be supplied by a service to support pagination?

Answer:

In addition to the actual data, a service must provide pagination specific information like total number of records, number of records per page, total number of pages, current page number, etc. Clients can use this information to determine the current state as well as construct a URL to fetch the previous or next pages. Services can also specify pagination information as a special Link header. The Link header consists of a set of links which can be used to scroll backwards or forward.

200: How can you sort the results returned by a REST service? Explain with some examples.

Answer:

Sorting allows REST clients to determine the order in which the results are returned by a REST service. REST services that support sorting allow clients to submit parameters with properties to be used for sorting. REST services can also allow clients to specify the sort direction, that is ascending or descending. For example, consider the following URIs:

```
http://personserver.com/personList?sort=firstname
```

Here, the URI has the sort parameter with the value as firstName which specifies that the client application wants the results to be sorted as per the firstName.

```
http://personserver.com/personList?sort=firstname,a
sc
```

Here, the URI has the sort parameter with the value as firstName and the value asc which specifies that the client application wants the results to be sorted as per the firstName in the ascending order

HR Interview Questions

Review these typical interview questions and think about how you would answer them. Read the answers listed; you will find best possible answers along with strategies and suggestions

1: Where do you find ideas?

Answer:

Ideas can come from all places, and an interviewer wants to see that your ideas are just as varied. Mention multiple places that you gain ideas from, or settings in which you find yourself brainstorming. Additionally, elaborate on how you record ideas or expand upon them later.

2: How do you achieve creativity in the workplace?

Answer:

It's important to show the interviewer that you're capable of being resourceful and innovative in the workplace, without stepping outside the lines of company values. Explain where ideas normally stem from for you (examples may include an exercise such as list-making or a mind map), and connect this to a particular task in your job that it would be helpful to be creative in.

3: How do you push others to create ideas?

Answer:

If you're in a supervisory position, this may be requiring employees to submit a particular number of ideas, or to complete regular idea-generating exercises, in order to work their creative muscles. However, you can also push others around you to create ideas simply by creating more of your own. Additionally, discuss with the interviewer the importance of questioning people as a way to inspire ideas and change.

4: Describe your creativity.

Answer:

Try to keep this answer within the professional realm, but if you have an impressive background in something creative outside of your employment history, don't be afraid to include it in your answer also. The best answers about creativity will relate problem-solving skills, goal-setting, and finding innovative ways to tackle a project or make a sale in the workplace. However, passions outside of the office are great, too (so long as they don't cut into your work time or mental space).

5: Ten years ago, what were your career goals?

Answer:

In reflecting back to what your career goals were ten years ago, it's important to show the ways in which you've made progress in that time. Draw distinct links between specific objectives that you've achieved, and speak candidly about how it felt to reach those goals. Remain positive, upbeat, and growth-oriented, even if you haven't yet achieved all of the goals you set out to reach.

6: Tell me about a weakness you used to have, and how you changed it.

Answer:

Choose a non-professional weakness that you used to have, and outline the process you went through in order to grow past it. Explain the weakness itself, why it was problematic, the action steps you planned, how you achieved them, and the end result.

7: Tell me about your goal-setting process.

Answer:

When describing your goal-setting process, clearly outline the way that you create an outline for yourself. It may be helpful to offer an example of a particular goal you've set in the past, and use this as a starting point to guide the way you created action steps, check-in points, and how the goal was eventually achieved.

8: Tell me about a time when you solved a problem by creating actionable steps to follow.

Answer:

This question will help the interviewer to see how you talented you are in outlining, problem resolution, and goal-setting. Explain thoroughly the procedure of outlining the problem, establishing steps to take, and then how you followed the steps (such as through check-in points along the way, or intermediary goals).

9: Where do you see yourself five years from now?

Answer:

Have some idea of where you would like to have advanced to in the position you're applying for, over the next several years. Make sure that your future plans line up with you still working for the company, and stay positive about potential advancement. Focus on future opportunities, and what you're looking forward to – but make sure your reasons for advancement are admirable, such as greater experience and the chance to learn, rather than simply being out for a higher salary.

10: When in a position, do you look for opportunities to promote?

Answer:

There's a fine balance in this question – you want to show the interviewer that you have initiative and motivation to advance in your career, but not at the expense of appearing opportunistic or selfishly-motivated. Explain that you are always open to growth opportunities, and very willing to take on new responsibilities as your career advances.

11: On a scale of 1 to 10, how successful has your life been?

Answer:

Though you may still have a long list of goals to achieve, it's important to keep this answer positively-focused. Choose a high number between 7 and 9, and explain that you feel your life has been largely successful and satisfactory as a result of several specific achievements or experiences. Don't go as high as a 10, as the interviewer may not believe your response or in your ability to reason critically.

12: What is your greatest goal in life?

Answer:

It's okay for this answer to stray a bit into your personal life, but best if you can keep it professionally-focused. While specific goals are great, if your personal goal doesn't match up exactly with one of the company's objectives, you're better off keeping your goal a little more generic and encompassing, such as "success in my career" or "leading a happy and fulfilling life." Keep your answer brief, and show a decisive nature – most importantly, make it clear that you've already thought about this question and know what you want.

13: Tell me about a time when you set a goal in your personal life and achieved it.

Answer:

The interviewer can see that you excel at setting goals in your professional life, but he or she also wants to know that you are consistent in your life and capable of setting goals outside of the office as well. Use an example such as making a goal to eat more healthily or to drink more water, and discuss what steps you outlined to achieve your goal, the process of taking action, and the final results as well.

14: What is your greatest goal in your career?

Answer:

Have a very specific goal of something you want to achieve in your career in mind, and be sure that it's something the position clearly puts you in line to accomplish. Offer the goal as well as your plans to get there, and emphasize clear ways in which this position will be an opportunity to work toward the goal.

15: Tell me about a time when you achieved a goal.

Answer:

Start out with how you set the goal, and why you chose it. Then, take the interviewer through the process of outlining the goal, taking steps to achieve it, the outcome, and finally, how you felt after achieving it or recognition you received. The most important part of this question includes the planning and implementation of strategies, so focus most of your time on explaining these aspects. However, the preliminary decisions and end results are also important, so make sure to include them as well.

16: What areas of your work would you still like to improve in? What are your plans to do this?

Answer:

While you may not want the interviewer to focus on things you could improve on, it's important to be self-aware of your own growth opportunities. More importantly, you can impress an interviewer by having specific goals and actions outlined in order to facilitate your growth, even if your area of improvement is something as simple as increasing sales or finding new ways to create greater efficiency.

17: Tell me about your favorite book or newspaper.

Answer:

The interviewer will look at your answer to this question in order to determine your ability to analyze and review critically. Additionally, try to choose something that is on a topic related to your field or that embodies a theme important to your work, and be able to explain how it relates. Stay away from controversial subject matter, such as politics or religion.

18: If you could be rich or famous, which would you choose?

Answer:

This question speaks to your ability to think creatively, but your answer may also give great insight to your character. If you answer rich, your interviewer may interpret that you are self-

166   *RESTful Java Web Services Interview Questions You'll Most Likely Be Asked*

confident and don't seek approval from others, and that you like to be rewarded for your work. If you choose famous, your interviewer may gather that you like to be well-known and to deal with people, and to have the platform to deliver your message to others. Either way, it's important to back up your answer with sound reasoning.

19: If you could trade places with anyone for a week, who would it be and why?

Answer:

This question is largely designed to test your ability to think on your feet, and to come up with a reasonable answer to an outside the box question. Whoever you choose, explain your answer in a logical manner, and offer specific professional reasons that led you to choose the individual.

20: What would you say if I told you that just from glancing over your resume, I can already see three spelling mistakes?

Answer:

Clearly, your resume should be absolutely spotless – and you should be confident that it is. If your interviewer tries to make you second-guess yourself here, remain calm and poised and assert with a polite smile that you would be quite surprised as you are positive that your resume is error-free.

21: Tell me about your worldview.

Answer:

This question is designed to offer insight into your personality, so be aware of how the interviewer will interpret your answer. Speak

facebook.com/vibrantpublishers

openly and directly, and try to incorporate your own job skills into your outlook on life. For example, discuss your beliefs on the ways that hard work and dedication can always bring success, or in how learning new things is one of life's greatest gifts. It's okay to expand into general life principles here, but try to keep your thoughts related to the professional field as well.

22: What is the biggest mistake someone could make in an interview?

Answer:

The biggest mistake that could be made in an interview is to be caught off guard! Make sure that you don't commit whatever you answer here, and additionally be prepared for all questions. Other common mistakes include asking too early in the hiring process about job benefits, not having questions prepared when the interviewer asks if you have questions, arriving late, dressing casually or sloppily, or showing ignorance of the position.

23: If you won the $50m lottery, what would you do with the money?

Answer:

While a question such as this may seem out of place in a job interview, it's important to display your creative thinking and your ability to think on the spot. It's also helpful if you choose something admirable, yet believable, to do with the money such as donate the first seventy percent to a charitable cause, and divide the remainder among gifts for friends, family, and of course, yourself.

24: Is there ever a time when honesty isn't appropriate in the workplace?

Answer:

This may be a difficult question, but the only time that honesty isn't appropriate in the workplace is perhaps when you're feeling anger or another emotion that is best kept to yourself. If this is the case, explain simply that it is best to put some thoughts aside, and clarify that the process of keeping some thoughts quiet is often enough to smooth over any unsettled emotions, thus eliminating the problem.

25: If you could travel anywhere in the world, where would it be?

Answer:

This question is meant to allow you to be creative – so go ahead and stretch your thoughts to come up with a unique answer. However, be sure to keep your answer professionally-minded. For example, choose somewhere rich with culture or that would expose you to a new experience, rather than going on an expensive cruise through the Bahamas.

26: What would I find in your refrigerator right now?

Answer:

An interviewer may ask a creative question such as this in order to discern your ability to answer unexpected questions calmly, or, to try to gain some insight into your personality. For example, candidates with a refrigerator full of junk food or take-out may be more likely to be under stress or have health issues, while a candidate with a balanced refrigerator full of nutritious staples may be more likely to lead a balanced mental life, as well.

27: If you could play any sport professionally, what would it be and what aspect draws you to it?

Answer:

Even if you don't know much about professional sports, this question might be a great opportunity to highlight some of your greatest professional working skills. For example, you may choose to play professional basketball, because you admire the teamwork and coordination that goes into creating a solid play. Or, you may choose to play professional tennis, because you consider yourself to be a go-getter with a solid work ethic and great dedication to perfecting your craft. Explain your choice simply to the interviewer without elaborating on drawn-out sports metaphors, and be sure to point out specific areas or skills in which you excel.

28: Who were the presidential and vice-presidential candidates in the 2008 elections?

Answer:

This question, plain and simple, is intended as a gauge of your intelligence and awareness. If you miss this question, you may well fail the interview. Offer your response with a polite smile, because you understand that there are some individuals who probably miss this question.

29: Explain X task in a few short sentences as you would to a second-grader.

Answer:

An interviewer may ask you to break down a normal job task that you would complete in a manner that a child could understand, in part to test your knowledge of the task's inner workings – but in larger part, to test your ability to explain a process in simple, basic terms. While you and your co-workers may be able to converse using highly technical language, being able to simplify a process is an important skill for any employee to have.

30: If you could compare yourself to any animal, what would it be?

Answer:

Many interviewers ask this question, and it's not to determine which character traits you think you embody – instead, the interviewer wants to see that you can think outside the box, and that you're able to reason your way through any situation. Regardless of what animal you answer, be sure that you provide a thorough reason for your choice.

31: Who is your hero?

Answer:

Your hero may be your mother or father, an old professor, someone successful in your field, or perhaps even Wonder Woman – but keep your reasoning for your choice professional, and be prepared to offer a logical train of thought. Choose someone who embodies values that are important in your chosen career field, and answer the question with a smile and sense of passion.

32: Who would play you in the movie about your life?

Answer:

As with many creative questions that challenge an interviewee to think outside the box, the answer to this question is not as important as how you answer it. Choose a professional, and relatively non-controversial actor or actress, and then be prepared to offer specific reasoning for your choice, employing important skills or traits you possess.

33: Name five people, alive or dead, that would be at your ideal dinner party.

Answer:

Smile and sound excited at the opportunity to think outside the box when asked this question, even if it seems to come from left field. Choose dynamic, inspiring individuals who you could truly learn from, and explain what each of them would have to offer to the conversation. Don't forget to include yourself, and to talk about what you would bring to the conversation as well!

34: What is the best way for a company to advertise?

Answer:

If you're going for a position in any career other than marketing, this question is probably intended to demonstrate your ability to think critically and to provide reflective support for your answers. As such, the particular method you choose is not so important as why you've chosen it. For example, word of mouth advertising is important because customers will inherently trust the source, and social media advertising is important as it reaches new customers quickly and cheaply.

35: Is it better to gain a new customer or to keep an old one?

Answer:

In almost every case, it is better to keep an old customer, and it's important that you are able to articulate why this is. First, new customers generally cost companies more than retaining old ones does, and new customers are more likely to switch to a different company. Additionally, keeping old customers is a great way to provide a stable backbone for the company, as well as to also gain new customers as they are likely to recommend your company to friends.

36: What is the best way to win clients from competitors?

Answer:

There are many schools of thought on the best way to win clients from competitors, and unless you know that your interviewer adheres to a specific thought or practice, it's best to keep this question general. Rather than using absolute language, focus on the benefits of one or two strategies and show a clear, critical understanding of how these ways can succeed in a practical application.

37: How do you feel about companies monitoring internet usage?

Answer:

Generally speaking, most companies will monitor some degree of internet usage over their employees – and during an interview is not the best time to rebel against this practice. Instead, focus on positive aspects such as the way it can lead to increased productivity for some employees who may be easily lost in the world of resourceful information available to them.

38: What is your first impression of our company?

Answer:

Obviously, this should be a positive answer! Pick out a couple key components of the company's message or goals that you especially identify with or that pertain to your experience, and discuss why you believe these missions are so important.

39: Tell me about your personal philosophy on business.

Answer:

Your personal philosophy on business should be well-thought out, and in line with the missions and objectives of the company. Stay focused on positive aspects such as the service it can provide, and the lessons people gain in business, and offer insight as to where your philosophy has come from.

40: What's most important in a business model: sales, customer service, marketing, management, etc.?

Answer:

For many positions, it may be a good strategy to tailor this answer to the type of field you're working in, and to explain why that aspect of business is key. However, by explaining that each aspect is integral to the function as a whole, you can display a greater sense of business savvy to the interviewer and may stand out in his or her mind as a particularly aware candidate.

41: How do you keep up with news and emerging trends in the field?

Answer:

The interviewer wants to see that you are aware of what's currently going on in your field. It is important that your education does not stop after college, and the most successful candidates will have a list of resources they regularly turn to already in place, so that they may stay aware and engaged in developing trends.

42: Would you have a problem adhering to company policies on social media?

Answer:

Social media concerns in the workplace have become a greater issue, and many companies now outline policies for the use of social media. Interviewers will want to be assured that you won't have a problem adhering to company standards, and that you will maintain a consistent, professional image both in the office and online.

43: Tell me about one of the greatest problems facing X industry today.

Answer:

If you're involved in your career field, and spend time on your own studying trends and new developments, you should be able to display an awareness of both problems and potential solutions coming up in the industry. Research some of the latest news before heading into the interview, and be prepared to discuss current events thoroughly.

44: What do you think it takes to be successful in our company?

Answer:

Research the company prior to the interview. Be aware of the company's mission and main objectives, as well as some of the biggest names in the company, and also keep in mind how they achieved success. Keep your answer focused on specific objectives you could reach in order to help the company achieve its goals.

45: What is your favorite part of working in this career field?

Answer:

This question is an opportunity to discuss some of your favorite aspects of the job, and to highlight why you are a great candidate for the particular position. Choose elements of the work you enjoy that are related to what you would do if hired for the position. Remember to remain enthusiastic and excited for the opportunities you could attain in the job.

46: What do you see happening to your career in the next 10 years?

Answer:

If you're plugged in to what's happening in your career now, and are making an effort to stay abreast of emerging trends in your field, you should be able to offer the interviewer several predictions as to where your career or field may be heading. This insight and level of awareness shows a level of dedication and interest that is important to employers.

47: What are the three most important things you're looking for in a position?

Answer:

The top three things you want in a position should be similar to the top three things the employer wants from an employee, so that it is clear that you are well-matched to the job. For example, the employer wants a candidate who is well-qualified for and has practical experience – and you want a position that allows you to use your education and skills to their best applications. The employer wants a candidate who is willing to take on new challenges and develop new systems to increase sales or productivity – and you want a position that pushes you and offers opportunities to develop, create, and lead new initiatives. The employer wants a candidate who will grow into and stay with the company for a long time – and you want a position that offers stability and believes in building a strong team. Research what the employer is looking for beforehand, and match your objectives to theirs.

48: How are you evaluating the companies you're looking to work with?

Answer:

While you may feel uncomfortable exerting your own requirements during the interview, the employer wants to see that you are thinking critically about the companies you're applying with, just as they are critically looking at you. Don't be afraid to specify what your needs from a company are (but do try to make sure they match up well with the company – preferably before you apply there), and show confidence and decisiveness in your answer. The interviewer wants to know that you're the kind of person who knows what they want, and how to get it.

49: Are you comfortable working for _____ salary?

Answer:

If the answer to this question is no, it may be a bit of a deal-breaker in a first interview, as you are unlikely to have much room to negotiate. You can try to leverage a bit by highlighting specific experience you have, and how that makes you qualified for more, but be aware that this is very difficult to navigate at this step of the process. To avoid this situation, be aware of industry standards and, if possible, company standards, prior to your application.

50: Why did you choose your last job?

Answer:

In learning what led you to your last job, the interviewer is able to get a feel for the types of things that motivate you. Keep these professionally-focused, and remain passionate about the early points of your career, and how excited you were to get started in the field.

51: How long has it been since your last job and why?

Answer:

Be sure to have an explanation prepared for all gaps in employment, and make sure it's a professional reason. Don't mention difficulties you may have had in finding a job, and instead focus on positive things such as pursuing outside interests or perhaps returning to school for additional education.

52: What other types of jobs have you been looking for?

Answer:

The answer to this question can show the interviewer that you're both on the market and in demand. Mention jobs you've applied for or looked at that are closely related to your field, or similar to the position you're interviewing for. Don't bring up last-ditch efforts that found you applying for a part-time job completely unrelated to your field.

53: Have you ever been disciplined at work?

Answer:

Hopefully the answer here is no – but if you have been disciplined for something at work though, be absolutely sure that you can explain it thoroughly. Detail what you learned from the situation, and reflect on how you grew after the process.

54: What is your availability like?

Answer:

Your availability should obviously be as open as possible, and any gaps in availability should be explained and accounted for. Avoid asking about vacation or personal days (as well as other benefits), and convey to the interviewer how serious you are about your work.

55: May I contact your current employer?

Answer:

If possible, it is best to allow an interviewer to contact your current employer as a reference. However, if it's important that your employer is not contacted, explain your reason tactfully, such as you just started job searching and you haven't had the opportunity yet to inform them that you are looking for other employment. Be careful of this reasoning though, as employers may wonder if you'll start shopping for something better while employed with them as well.

56: Do you have any valuable contacts you could bring to our business?

Answer:

It's great if you can bring knowledge, references, or other contacts that your new employer may be able to network with. However, be sure that you aren't offering up any of your previous employer's clients, or in any way violating contractual agreements.

57: How soon would you be available to start working?

Answer:

While you want to be sure that you're available to start as soon as possible if the company is interested in hiring you, if you still have another job, be sure to give them at least two weeks' notice. Though your new employer may be anxious for you to start, they will want to hire a worker whom they can respect for giving adequate notice, so that they won't have to worry if you'll eventually leave them in the lurch.

58: Why would your last employer say that you left?

Answer:

The key to this question is that your employer's answer must be the same as your own answer about why you left. For instance, if you've told your employer that you left to find a position with greater opportunities for career advancement, your employer had better not say that you were let go for missing too many days of work. Honesty is key in your job application process.

59: How long have you been actively looking for a job?

Answer:

It's best if you haven't been actively looking for a job for very long, as a long period of time may make the interviewer wonder why no one else has hired you. If it has been awhile, make sure to explain why, and keep it positive. Perhaps you haven't come across many opportunities that provide you with enough of a challenge or that are adequately matched to someone of your education and experience.

60: When don't you show up to work?

Answer:

Clearly, the only time acceptable to miss work is for a real emergency or when you're truly sick – so don't start bringing up times now that you plan to miss work due to vacations or family birthdays. Alternatively, you can tell the interviewer how dedicated to your work you are, and how you always strive to be fully present and to put in the same amount of work every time you come in, even when you're feeling slightly under the weather.

61: What is the most common reason you miss work?

Answer:

If there is a reason that you will miss work routinely, this is the time to disclose it – but doing so during an interview will reflect negatively on you. Ideally, you will only miss work during cases of extreme illness or other emergencies.

62: What is your attendance record like?

Answer:

Be sure to answer this question honestly, but ideally you will have already put in the work to back up the fact that you rarely miss days or arrive late. However, if there are gaps in your attendance, explain them briefly with appropriate reasons, and make sure to emphasize your dedication to your work, and reliability.

63: Where did you hear about this position?

Answer:

This may seem like a simple question, but the answer can actually speak volumes about you. If you were referred by a friend or another employee who works for the company, this is a great chance to mention your connection (if the person is in good standing!). However, if you heard about it from somewhere like a career fair or a work placement agency, you may want to focus on how pleased you were to come across such a wonderful opportunity.

64: Tell me anything else you'd like me to know when making a hiring decision.

Answer:

This is a great opportunity for you to give a final sell of yourself to the interviewer – use this time to remind the interviewer of why you are qualified for the position, and what you can bring to the company that no one else can. Express your excitement for the opportunity to work with a company pursuing X mission.

65: Why would your skills be a good match with X objective of our company?

Answer:

If you've researched the company before the interview, answering this question should be no problem. Determine several of the company's main objectives, and explain how specific skills that you have are conducive to them. Also, think about ways that your experience and skills can translate to helping the company expand upon these objectives, and to reach further goals. If your old company had a similar objective, give a specific example of how you helped the company to meet it.

66: What do you think this job entails?

Answer:

Make sure you've researched the position well before heading into the interview. Read any and all job descriptions you can find (at best, directly from the employer's website or job posting), and make note of key duties, responsibilities, and experience required. Few things are less impressive to an interviewer than a candidate who has no idea what sort of job they're actually being interviewed for.

67: Is there anything else about the job or company you'd like to know?

Answer:

If you have learned about the company beforehand, this is a great opportunity to show that you put in the effort to study before the interview. Ask questions about the company's mission in relation to current industry trends, and engage the interviewer in interesting, relevant conversation. Additionally, clear up anything else you need to know about the specific position before leaving – so that if the interviewer calls with an offer, you'll be prepared to answer.

68: Are you the best candidate for this position?

Answer:

Yes! Offer specific details about what makes you qualified for this position, and be sure to discuss (and show) your unbridled passion and enthusiasm for the new opportunity, the job, and the company.

69: How did you prepare for this interview?

Answer:

The key part of this question is to make sure that you have prepared! Be sure that you've researched the company, their objectives, and their services prior to the interview, and know as much about the specific position as you possibly can. It's also helpful to learn about the company's history and key players in the current organization.

70: If you were hired here, what would you do on your first day?

Answer:

While many people will answer this question in a boring fashion, going through the standard first day procedures, this question is actually a great chance for you to show the interviewer why you will make a great hire. In addition to things like going through training or orientation, emphasize how much you would enjoy meeting your supervisors and coworkers, or how you would spend a lot of the day asking questions and taking in all of your new surroundings.

71: Have you viewed our company's website?

Answer:

Clearly, you should have viewed the company's website and done some preliminary research on them before coming to the interview. If for some reason you did not, do not say that you did, as the interviewer may reveal you by asking a specific question about it. If you did look at the company's website, this is an appropriate time to bring up something you saw there that was of particular interest to you, or a value that you especially supported.

72: How does X experience on your resume relate to this position?

Answer:

Many applicants will have some bit of experience on their resume that does not clearly translate to the specific job in question. However, be prepared to be asked about this type of seemingly-irrelevant experience, and have a response prepared that takes into account similar skill sets or training that the two may share.

73: Why do you want this position?

Answer:

Keep this answer focused positively on aspects of this specific job that will allow you to further your skills, offer new experience, or that will be an opportunity for you to do something that you particularly enjoy. Don't tell the interviewer that you've been looking for a job for a long time, or that the pay is very appealing, or you will appear unmotivated and opportunistic.

74: How is your background relevant to this position?

Answer:

Ideally, this should be obvious from your resume. However, in instances where your experience is more loosely-related to the position, make sure that you've researched the job and company well before the interview. That way, you can intelligently relate the experience and skills that you do have, to similar skills that would be needed in the new position. Explain specifically how your skills will translate, and use words to describe your background such as "preparation" and "learning." Your prospective position should be described as an "opportunity" and a chance for "growth and development."

75: How do you feel about X mission of our company?

Answer:

It's important to have researched the company prior to the interview – and if you've done so, this question won't catch you off guard. The best answer is one that is simple, to the point, and shows knowledge of the mission at hand. Offer a few short statements as to why you believe in the mission's importance, and note that you would be interested in the chance to work with a company that supports it.

INDEX

RESTful Java Web Services Interview Questions

Java REST APIs and Implementations

21: What are the options available to develop RESTful services in Java?

22: Name some implementations of the JAX-RS API and explain.

23: What are the differences between Jersey and RESTEasy?

24: What is the difference between Jersey and Spring REST?

25: What is Jackson?

26: What is JAXB?

27: What is RESTlet?

28: What are the steps in building a REST application that uses Jersey in Eclipse?

29: What are the advantages of Spring REST?

30: Can Jersey be used with Spring? If so, how?

JAX–RS Basics

31: Which Java API is used for building a REST service?

32: What are the advantages of the JAX-RS specification?

33: Which JAX-RS annotations map to the HTTP methods?

34: Write a code sample that demonstrates a REST method that processes a GET request.

35: Write a sample code that demonstrates saving a custom object via REST.

36: What is HTTP content negotiation and how is it handled by JAX-RS?

37: Which classes are available in JAX-RS framework that help to implement the HATEOAS principle?

38: What is the use of the `@Produces` and `@Consumes` annotations?

39: How does client request matching work?

JAX-RS Request Handling

40: What is the use of the `@Path` annotation?

41: Write a code sample that uses the `@PathParam` annotation.

42: What is the difference between `@QueryParam` and `@PathParam`?

43: What is the use of the `@HeaderParam` annotation? Explain with an example.

44: Which annotation should be used to consolidate input parameters to a JAX-RS method? Explain with a code sample.

45: What is the `@CookieParam` annotation used for?

46: What is the use of the `@DefaultValue` annotation?

47: How are matrix parameters different from query parameters?

JAX-RS Response Handling

48: Write a code sample that demonstrates a REST method that returns data in plain text format.

49: Explain the `javax.ws.rs.core.Response` class and what it is used for.

50: What is the `ResponseBuilder` class? Explain with a code sample.

51: What is the use of the `Response.created` method?

52: How can you create a `Response` object with a particular status code?

53: What is the use of the `Response.readEntity` method? Explain with a code sample.

54: What is the difference between `getHeaderString` and `getStringHeaders` method?

55: Write a code sample that demonstrates the `@Produces` annotation.

56: Write a code sample that demonstrates the `@Consumes` annotation.

57: What is the use of the `Response.ok` method?

JAX-RS Exception Handling

58: How does exception handling work in a REST application?

59: What is the use of javax.ws.rs.WebApplicationException?

60: Write a code sample that demonstrates an `ExceptionMapper` for a custom exception.

61: What is the `ForbiddenException`?

62: How can you create a `WebApplicationException` instance?

63: Explain the `NotFoundException` and write a sample code that throws this exception.

64: Which exception will be thrown when there is no JAX-RS method that produces the media type specified in the accept request header?

JAX-RS Client

65: What are the ways in which you can create a REST client application?

66: What is the use of the `javax.ws.rs.client.ClientBuilder` interface?

67: What is the use of the `javax.ws.rs.client.Client` interface?

68: Explain the purpose of the `WebTarget` interface.

69: How can you use `WebTarget` to resolve a path parameter? Explain with a code sample.

70: What are the steps in creating an `Invocation.Builder` to invoke a REST service?

71: What is the use of the `WebTarget.queryParam` method? Explain with a code sample.

72: Explain the `Invocation.Builder` interface.

73: Write a sample code that demonstrates how to create a client application that queries a REST service.

JAX-RS Filters

74: What are the types of filters that can be specified in a REST application?

75: What is the use of a server side or client side filter?

76: Explain the types of server side filters.

77: What are the `@PreMatching` and `@PostMatching` annotations used for?

78: What is the `ContainerResponseFilter` interface?

79: Write a code sample that demonstrates how the `ContainerRequestFilter` can be used to filter the incoming request.

80: What is the use of the `ContainerRequestContext` interface?

81: Write a code sample that demonstrates the `ContainerResponseFilter` interface.

82: Explain the `ClientRequestFilter` interface with a code sample.

83: Write a code sample that demonstrates how a client side response filter should be implemented.

JAX-RS Asynchronous Processing

84: How does asynchronous request processing work in JAX-RS? Explain the important classes that are used in asynchronous processing.

85: Explain the `AsyncInvoker` interface and write a code sample that uses this interface to invoke a GET method asynchronously.

86: How can a JAX-RS client that sends an asynchronous request process the response via a Callback?

87: Explain the differences between using the polling approach and callback approach.

88: What is the advantage of asynchronous server side processing?

89: How can asynchronous processing be applied on the server side?

JAX-RS Security

90: How can you enforce authentication and authorization for a JAX-RS method?

91: What are the steps in setting up authentication and authorization information in web.xml?

92: What are the different ways of setting up authorization in a JAX-RS application? Explain which is a better way to setup authorization.

93: What is the use of the `@RolesAllowed` annotation?

94: What is the use of the `javax.ws.rs.core.SecurityContext` interface?

JAX-RS Miscellaneous

95: What is the use of the `Link` and `Link.Builder` classes?

96: How does JAX-RS support caching?

97: What is the use of the `javax.ws.rs.core.EntityTag` class?

98: How can you use Java's built in HTTP client library to connect to a REST service?

99: What are interceptors in the context of a JAX-RS application?

100: What is the use of the `javax.ws.rs.core.Request` class?

Spring REST Basics

101: Name some of the important annotations that are required while implementing a REST application via Spring.

102: What are the steps involved in creating a REST application via Spring?

103: Elaborate the `@Controller` annotation.

104: Explain the differences between `@Controller` and `@RestController`.

105: How can you specify the URI that a method in a Controller maps to?

106: What is the use of the `RequestParam` annotation? Write a code sample which demonstrates it.

107: What is the use of the `@RequestBody` and `@ResponseBody` annotations?

108: What is an `HttpMessageConverter` used for in Spring REST?

109: How does Spring REST support the HATEOAS REST principle?

Spring REST Request Processing

110: Explain the attributes of the `@RequestMapping` annotation.

111: What will happen if the method attribute is not specified with the `@RequestMapping` annotation?

112: Explain the `@GetMapping` annotations.

113: Explain the differences between `@RequestMapping` and `@PostMapping`.

114: Write a sample code that handles a Get request via Spring REST.

115: Explain the differences between `@Get` annotation and `@GetMapping` annotation.

116: What is the use of the `@PathVariable` annotation?

117: Explain the differences between `@PathVariable` and `@RequestParam` annotations.

118: How can you specify multiple URI paths with a `@RequestMapping` annotation?

119: What is the use of the headers attribute in the `@GetMapping` annotation? Explain with an example.

120: How can you specify a default value for a request parameter?

Explain with a code sample.

Spring REST Response Processing

121: What is the use of the `ResponseEntity` class?

122: Write a code sample that demonstrates the `@RequestBody` annotation.

123: When can the `@ResponseBody` annotation be skipped?

124: What is the `ResponseEntity.BodyBuilder` interface?

125: What is the use of the `ResponseEntity.ok` method? Write a code sample that demonstrates this method.

126: How can you create a `ResponseEntity` with a particular status code?

127: Write a code sample that demonstrates how you can set a header in a `ResponseEntity` class.

128: Write a code sample that demonstrates a Spring REST method that produces a text response.

129: What is the use of the `@ResponseStatus` annotation?

130: What is the use of the `consumes` attribute on the `@RequestMapping` annotation? Explain with a code sample.

Spring REST Exception Handling

131: What are the different ways in which you can achieve exception handling in a Spring REST application?

132: Explain with a code sample how exception handling can be done via the `@ExceptionHandler` annotation.

133: Write a code sample that demonstrates how the `@ResponseStatus` annotation can be used to send an error corresponding to HTTP status code 500.

134: What are the limitations on using the `@ExceptionHandler` annotation for handling exceptions in a Spring REST application? How can you overcome these limitations?

135: What are the types or arguments that can be passed to a method that has the `@ExceptionHandler` annotation and what should be the return type of such a method?

136: What are the advantages of `ResponseStatusException`?

137: Write a code sample that demonstrates how you can do exception handling via the `ResponseStatusException`.

138: How can `@ControllerAdvice` be used to handle exceptions? Explain with a code sample.

139: What is the use of the `ResponseEntityExceptionHandler`?

140: What is the `MediaTypeNotSupportedException`?

Spring REST Client

141: What are the different ways in which you can create a client application for a Spring REST service?

142: What is the use of the `RestTemplate` class?

143: Write a code sample that demonstrates the `RestTemplate.getForEntity` method.

144: How can a Spring REST client application retrieve header information? Explain with a code sample.

145: How can you specify parameter values while performing an HTTP GET in a Spring REST client application?

146: What is the difference between the `postForEntity`, `postForObject` and `postForLocation` methods?

147: What is the use of the `RequestEntity` class?

148: Write a sample code that demonstrates how you can perform a delete operation via a Spring REST client.

149: What is the use of the `resttemplate.exchange` method?

150: Explain the `WebClient` interface.

JSON

151: What is JSON? Why was it developed?

152: Explain the main features of JSON due to which developers prefer to use it.

153: What are the similarities between JSON and XML?

154: What are the differences between JSON and XML?

155: What are the data types supported by JSON?

156: Explain JSON syntax.

157: Explain the JSON object syntax in detail.

158: Explain the JSON array syntax in detail.

159: What limitations does JSON have?

160: Write a code sample that demonstrates a Java class and the corresponding JSON value for it.

161: Write a Java class that corresponds to a Book object with fields for book id, book name and a List of values corresponding to book authors. Also write the JSON String that stores this information for the book with id=1, name="Book1" and authors as "Author1", "Author2".

162: Write a code sample that demonstrates how you can represent a `List` of objects via JSON.

163: Write a sample code that shows how you can represent a nested object in JSON.

Postman

164: List some tools that are commonly used for testing a REST service.

165: What is Postman?

166: How can you test the following REST method in Postman?

167: Explain the term, Collection, in Postman.

168: What is the use of an environment variable in Postman?

169: How can you test all the methods in a Spring REST controller at once in Postman?

170: How can you define the sequence in which requests will be run by a Collection Runner?

171: How can you test the following JAX-RS REST code request via Postman?

172: How can you specify authentication credentials via Postman?

173: What is a Mock server in Postman?

174: Write a JAX-RS method that accepts a cookie and also explain how such a method will be tested in Postman.

175: How can you use Postman to check if a REST method returns 200 OK status code?

Swagger

Miscellaneous

198: How can you achieve pagination in a REST application?

199: In addition to the actual data, what data must be supplied by a
     service to support pagination?

200: How can you sort the results returned by a REST service?

HR Interview Questions

what aspect draws you to it?

28: Who were the presidential and vice-presidential candidates in the 2008 elections?

29: Explain X task in a few short sentences as you would to a second-grader.

30: If you could compare yourself to any animal, what would it be?

31: Who is your hero?

32: Who would play you in the movie about your life?

33: Name five people, alive or dead, that would be at your ideal dinner party.

34: What is the best way for a company to advertise?

35: Is it better to gain a new customer or to keep an old one?

36: What is the best way to win clients from competitors?

37: How do you feel about companies monitoring internet usage?

38: What is your first impression of our company?

39: Tell me about your personal philosophy on business.

40: What's most important in a business model: sales, customer service, marketing, management, etc.?

41: How do you keep up with news and emerging trends in the field?

42: Would you have a problem adhering to company policies on social media?

43: Tell me about one of the greatest problems facing *X industry* today.

44: What do you think it takes to be successful in our company?

45: What is your favorite part of working in this career field?

46: What do you see happening to your career in the next 10 years?

47: 4What are the three most important things you're looking for in a position?

48: How are you evaluating the companies you're looking to work with?

49: Are you comfortable working for _____ salary?

50: Why did you choose your last job?

51: How long has it been since your last job and why?

52: What other types of jobs have you been looking for?

53: Have you ever been disciplined at work?

Some of the following titles might also be handy:

1. .NET Interview Questions You'll Most Likely Be Asked
2. 200 Interview Questions You'll Most Likely Be Asked
3. Access VBA Programming Interview Questions You'll Most Likely Be Asked
4. Adobe ColdFusion Interview Questions You'll Most Likely Be Asked
5. Advanced C++ Interview Questions You'll Most Likely Be Asked
6. Advanced Excel Interview Questions You'll Most Likely Be Asked
7. Advanced JAVA Interview Questions You'll Most Likely Be Asked
8. Advanced SAS Interview Questions You'll Most Likely Be Asked
9. AJAX Interview Questions You'll Most Likely Be Asked
10. Algorithms Interview Questions You'll Most Likely Be Asked
11. Android Development Interview Questions You'll Most Likely Be Asked
12. Ant & Maven Interview Questions You'll Most Likely Be Asked
13. Apache Web Server Interview Questions You'll Most Likely Be Asked
14. Artificial Intelligence Interview Questions You'll Most Likely Be Asked
15. ASP.NET Interview Questions You'll Most Likely Be Asked
16. Automated Software Testing Interview Questions You'll Most Likely Be Asked
17. Base SAS Interview Questions You'll Most Likely Be Asked
18. BEA WebLogic Server Interview Questions You'll Most Likely Be Asked
19. C & C++ Interview Questions You'll Most Likely Be Asked
20. C# Interview Questions You'll Most Likely Be Asked
21. CCNA Interview Questions You'll Most Likely Be Asked
22. Cloud Computing Interview Questions You'll Most Likely Be Asked
23. Computer Architecture Interview Questions You'll Most Likely Be Asked
24. Computer Networks Interview Questions You'll Most Likely Be Asked
25. Core JAVA Interview Questions You'll Most Likely Be Asked
26. Data Structures & Algorithms Interview Questions You'll Most Likely Be Asked
27. EJB 3.0 Interview Questions You'll Most Likely Be Asked
28. Entity Framework Interview Questions You'll Most Likely Be Asked
29. Fedora & RHEL Interview Questions You'll Most Likely Be Asked
30. Hadoop BIG DATA Interview Questions You'll Most Likely Be Asked
31. Hibernate, Spring & Struts Interview Questions You'll Most Likely Be Asked
32. HTML, XHTML and CSS Interview Questions You'll Most Likely Be Asked
33. HTML5 Interview Questions You'll Most Likely Be Asked
34. IBM WebSphere Application Server Interview Questions You'll Most Likely Be Asked
35. iOS SDK Interview Questions You'll Most Likely Be Asked
36. Java / J2EE Design Patterns Interview Questions You'll Most Likely Be Asked
37. Java / J2EE Interview Questions You'll Most Likely Be Asked
38. JavaScript Interview Questions You'll Most Likely Be Asked
39. JavaServer Faces Interview Questions You'll Most Likely Be Asked
40. JDBC Interview Questions You'll Most Likely Be Asked
41. jQuery Interview Questions You'll Most Likely Be Asked
42. JSP-Servlet Interview Questions You'll Most Likely Be Asked
43. JUnit Interview Questions You'll Most Likely Be Asked
44. Linux Interview Questions You'll Most Likely Be Asked

For complete list visit

www.vibrantpublishers.com

NOTES

Printed in Great Britain
by Amazon

18737626R00119